Enjoy

GOD'S IMPROVED PRESENCE!

A GUIDEBOOK ON THE HOLY SPIRIT
FOR INDIVIDUAL OR GROUP USE

By

RODNEY A. KVAMME

Box 152
Seeley Lake, MT 59868
(406) 677-2017

1988

Other books by Rodney A. Kvamme include:
Profiles of the Christ
(We See Jesus . . .)
Careless and Loving It!
(Clues for Living from
The Confessions of a Happy Pastor)
Miracles Today
(Understanding How God
Participates in Our Lives)

Copyright 1988 by Rodney A. Kvamme

First Edition - First Printing

Printed in the United States

ISBN 0-918292-16-6

Cover Design by Jeanne Moon
Composition by Richard Potter

Printed by
GRIGGS PRINTING & PUBLISHING
BOX 1351, HAVRE, MT 59501

Dedicated to the
Third Person in the Trinity
(The Other Two Will Understand)

*F*oreword

This book is one of many that have grown out of the fresh interest in the work of the Holy Spirit in most of the major non-pentecostal churches. Without disclaiming the traditions of the sacramental and liturgical forms of the Spirit's ministry, Pastor Kvamme calls us to examine what God may be telling us in this recent widespread concern with the movement of the Spirit. He writes out of his own thirty years as a parish pastor and military chaplain. Both from the Old Testament and the New, and especially from the life of Jesus and the witness of the apostle Paul, he points to truths that the church has always embraced, but not always taken as seriously as it might have.

No Christian can read it without serious, sometimes troubled, self-examination. Have we ignored gifts that God is eager to give us? Have we been indifferent to the power and joy and comfort that might have been ours? Have love of God and service to the neighbor eluded us because of our caution or disbelief? Could the fellowship in the congregation be the richer if we became more open to the prodding of the Spirit?

This book will deepen our trust in God; it will give boldness and expectation to our prayers; it will enrich our fellowship in the church. Besides being a blessing to the individual reader, with the helps offered in an appendix it can be a splendid tool for group study and edification. The book is itself a gift of the Spirit.

Alvin N. Rogness
President Emeritus
Luther Theological Seminary

Table
of
Contents

1. It's a Bird!.. 1

2. It's a Pain!..8

3. The Holy Spirit in the Life of Jesus.................21

4. The Holy Spirit in the Life of the Church
   ...He Calls.. 33

5. The Holy Spirit in the Life of the Church
   ...He Gathers... 44

6. The Holy Spirit in the Life of the Church
   ...He Enlightens with His Gifts.................50

7. The Holy Spirit in the Life of the Church
   ...He Sanctifies...62

8. The Holy Spirit in the Life of the Church
   ...He Keeps...72

9. The Holy Spirit in the Life of the Believer....81

Appendix: "Think...Talk...Pray About"...................88
   ...For Personal Reflection or Group Discussion

CHAPTER ONE

*I*t's A Bird!

How do you picture the Holy Spirit?

A Christian missionary had been teaching new Chinese disciples about the truth of the Trinity. At the close of the session, one young man came by the teacher, bowed very courteously, but with a quizzical look said, "Honorable Father, I understand. Honorable Son, I understand. But honorable Bird, I do not understand!"

Many old and young Christians alike are unclear about the third component of the Holy Trinity...some kind of strange bird, but honorable for sure.

The Scriptures, in a way, invite the problem. From among all creatures, the dove was chosen to symbolize the Holy Spirit. One problem results: a bird is an "it", and not a person. In a review of one recent book on the Holy Spirit, even a recognized theologian consistently referred to the third person of the Trinity as "it."

CLIPPED WINGS

What do you do with a bird so that it doesn't fly away? One tactic is to clip its wings. In ancient Greece, the goddess of victory had wings. In Athens, however, there is a temple dedicated to wingless victory. Someone got the idea that victory would permanently reside in Athens if her wings were clipped. There is always the temptation within the church to

1

do the same job on the Holy Spirit. Clip his wings so that he remains on the premises, at least within range. Clip his wings so that he does not get out of control and fly at will.

We had a pet pigeon for a while when our boys were small. It was only a little squab when we found it in a barn loft and brought it home. Pidgie presented no problems until it began to use its wings. There had to be a method devised to control its flight. The boys solved the problem with some string and a bolt. Pidgie was able to get off the ground all right, but the weight of the bolt limited the time it could be airborne. As Pidgie grew, more bolts were added to the aerial leash. We, and not Pidgie, determined how far, fast, and high the bird would fly. Can you imagine the church trying to make the Holy Spirit into some kind of wingless victory or fettered Pidgie?

By the way, Pidgie became too much of a problem to have around. We didn't want to turn the bird loose because we didn't know if it could take care of itself. Then the perfect solution materialized. A traveling circus came to town. It had a children's exhibit of common birds and animals.. but it didn't have a pigeon! When the show left town, Pidgie was caged between unlikely neighbors. On the right was a raccoon, and on the left was a skunk!

A "GILDED" CAGE

This leads me to a second method of keeping a bird from flying away— caging it. There are several cages that have been utilized in an attempt to "properly" contain the Holy Spirit. Sacramental churches have sought to use a "gilded" cage. The Holy Spirit is largely restricted to operating within the confines of Holy Baptism. Accordingly, if there is any work of the Spirit to be done, it must happen in connection with this sacrament. Baptism is, of course, a very significant area of the Spirit's operation, but it is regrettable when only limited flight of the Holy Spirit is permitted outside this gilded cage.

"May the Spirit inspire faith?" Well, yes, for Paul does write in 1st Corinthians 12 that "...no one can say 'Jesus is Lord' except by the Holy Spirit."

"May the Spirit propagate the fruits listed in Galatians 5?" I guess so, for there are no rules against love, joy, peace, etc.

"And may the Spirit freely bestow the gifts as mentioned in 1st Corinthians 12?" Too often, this question prompts many in the church to make no comment or even to begin checking the door and bars on the gilded cage!

If one gilded cage is indeed employed to house the Spirit within sacramental churches, then surely another cage should be allowed, namely, confirmation. Whether looked upon as sacrament or rite, the action of the Spirit should have top billing here. I cannot vouch for what has happened in other churches where confirmation is practiced, but in the Lutheran Church the Spirit has often been given page two instead of front page attention. I say this because in an older hymnal, the "red" one, the first page of the confirmation liturgy placed the *confirmand* in the spotlight. It might be more appropriate to say "on the hot seat," instead of in the spotlight, because the emphasis was upon insuring a passing grade in catechization and a convincing confession concerning personal faith. Having made a good, grace-filled beginning at baptism, there was often a reversion to works-righteousness at the time of confirmation. The young people being confirmed were coached to say the right things and were admonished that their hearts and lives had better match their lips or else! Whatever peace or security about salvation had been experienced prior to confirmation, it was often lost in the routine panic and fear of that awful day of public reckoning!

Then came page two... the rest (really the best) of the story. "Almighty and everlasting God, who has vouchsafed to regenerate these thy servants by Water and the Spirit, and hast forgiven them all their sins: strengthen them, we beseech thee, with the *Holy Ghost*, the Comforter; and daily increase in them thy *manifold gifts* of grace: the spirit of wisdom and understanding; the spirit of counsel and might; the spirit of knowledge and of the fear of the Lord, now and forever; through Jesus Christ, thy Son, our Lord. Amen.

"(Then shall the candidates kneel, and the Minister shall

lay his hand, or hands, on the head of each and say the Prayer of Blessing.)

"The Father in Heaven, for Jesus' sake, renew and increase in thee *the gift of the Holy Ghost*, to thy strengthening in faith, to thy growth in grace, to thy patience in suffering, and to the blessed hope of everlasting life. (Each one confirmed shall say: Amen.)" Service Book and Hymnal, page 246.

Thus grace beautifully returned to steal the show. Hopefully confirmands were not still in a daze from their rigorous questioning on page one so they missed the gracious promises of the Spirit's abiding presence and power on page two. By rite, confirmation is the believer's moment of "baptism with the Holy Spirit" while the Sacrament of Holy Baptism is a mutual invasion of life by the Father, Son and Spirit. If there must be gilded cages for the Holy Spirit, then there ought to be at least two, namely, baptism and confirmation.

A "GIFTED" CAGE

While sacramental churches have provided a "gilded" cage for the Holy Spirit, Classic Pentecostalism has sought to put the Spirit in a "gifted" cage. That gifted cage is the manifestation of speaking in tongues. The action of the Spirit in creating faith is thus given minor attention compared to the more major action of the *person* who is to make a decision for Christ, accept him as Savior and Lord, give his life to Jesus, or in some other way bring about a total commitment. The fruits of the Spirit also become more the fruits of the *believer* who comes under a call to obedience that can easily become a legalism of "shouldas and gottas." Faith and fruit aside, the primary authenticating sign of the Holy Spirit, according to classic pentecostals, is gift, and specifically the gift of tongues. The Spirit can "apportion as he wills" any of the other gifts, but this gift of tongues is one which must be given to any "fully experienced" Christian. Having performed in this gifted cage, the Spirit may then be released to the business of bestowing other gifts as well.

A SHAKING OF THE CAGE

Neo-pentecostalism, or the "charismatic movement" which began in the 1960s, not without cages of its own, has nevertheless brought witness against gilded and gifted cages. On the one hand, the Holy Spirit has been sprung from the gilded cage of Holy Baptism. Many people with backgrounds in sacramental churches have experienced the Spirit's operation in their everyday lives as Christians and within the fellowship of small, and not so small, group gatherings. Sacramentalists, highly revering their initiation into the Body of Christ in Holy Baptism, have also come to treasure "baptism with the Holy Spirit" as an equipping, present reality.

Neo-pentecostalism has been a disturbance not only within sacramental churches. Classic pentecostals have been discombobulated by their hugging (if not kissing) cousins as the Spirit has also been sprung from the gifted cage of speaking in tongues. Oh, there have also been some "charismatics" who have secretly or openly thought that the *real* show of the Spirit is tongues. But there are plenty others who, without the particular gift of tongues, have given obvious witness to the authentic manifestation and gifts of the Spirit in their lives too. Consequently, some of the classic pentecostals have experienced the same kind of trauma as the early Jewish Christians who found that Gentiles were also objects of the Spirit's ministrations.

Consternation has abounded in the camps of sacramental and classic pentecostal churches. The Spirit has been flying free and people have been ducking, like when a parakeet is loose in the house. Some have longed for the bird to get locked up again. Others have been titillated by all the excitement. Still others have more calmly assessed the good and the bad of the situation. But at least a good number in the household have been awakened to the fact that something is going on. Some have found that a liberated Spirit is also a liberating Spirit, and new moments of spiritual meaning have been experienced.

WHY, THEN, A BIRD?

"It's a bird!" Well, not really. The Holy Spirit is neither "it" nor "bird." Then why did the Spirit descend in the form of a dove at Jesus' baptism? The first reason is *presence*. The visible dove emphasized the presence of God the Father with Jesus as his ministry began. Though Jesus was "Immanuel" (God with us), he also needed "Immanuel assurance" (God with him) at this moment. The dove was an assuring visual aid both for Jesus and for John the Baptist (John 1:32-34).

The second reason is *peace*. The dove has a long history as a symbol of peace. Noah sent the dove out of the ark to test whether the turbulence of the flood had subsided. When the dove returned with an olive leaf in its mouth, Noah knew that it would soon be safe to exit the ark and begin living once more upon the earth. The book of Leviticus lists turtle doves and pigeons as appropriate offerings for poor people to make in order to effect atonement for their sins. How appropriate, then, that a dove should identify the Prince of Peace. Our usual kind of peace in this world is a mix of security and insecurity. As an Air Force Chaplain, I served mostly in the Strategic Air Command. Its symbol is a mailed fist that holds quite a combination.. an olive branch and a bolt of lightning! "Peace is our Profession" is part of the logo that stresses an assured peace through the presence of enough power to inhibit attack by any enemy. It is typical of the complications involved in making and keeping peace in the world.

His peace, the peace of Jesus, invaded the market of the world scene as a new, untested brand. It is a "given" peace, not a "striven for" peace (John 14:27). Its center is the heart of individuals, not the conference tables of summit meetings. St. Paul testifies to it as a peace that is beyond understanding, but not beyond experiencing (Phil. 4:7). No bird of prey, the harmless and defenseless dove was a unique candidate for the task of symbolically connecting the world to that unique commodity offered by the Prince of Peace and administered by the Holy Spirit.

Other features make the dove an appropriate sign of the Spirit. It is a *creature of the air*, and one of the oldest Hebrew words for Spirit (Ruach) means "breath." The dove is a symbol of *free flight*. Its course is more easily traceable than the free-flowing wind which Jesus used as an illustration of the Spirit (John 3:8). Finally, the alighting dove, *coming from above*, is a reminder of the source of all our blessings which come from the Father of mercies who reigns above all heavens and earth.

MORE THAN A BIRD

Though symbolized by a dove, the Holy Spirit is no more a bird than the United States is an eagle. He must not be treated like one. He surely must not be the object of attempts to cage or control him. At best such attempts are both futile and funny, and at worst they are presumptuous and blasphemous.

Someone has said that happiness is like a butterfly. Pursue it, and it eludes you. Stop the pursuit, and it alights on your shoulder. Spiritual happiness is much the same. Pursue, seek to coerce or control the Holy Spirit, and he will let you struggle in such frustrating activity. But relax in the assurance that he will deal best with you according to his wisdom and power, and you will experience the abiding presence of the Holy Spirit, the true "Bird of Paradise" in your life.

* * *

Note the "Think/Talk/Pray about" section relating to Chapter 1.

CHAPTER TWO

*I*t's A Pain!

When something is truly good, it should solve problems and not create them. If you begin with this premise, it is then disturbing to witness pain and division arising from people's varied understanding and experience of the Holy Spirit and his gifts. Have you wondered about such a situation?

CONGREGATIONS EXPERIENCE PAIN

The Holy Spirit is a pain. *The pain has been felt by congregations.*

Spiritual renewal involves such things as a fresh sense of forgiveness, a deeper assurance of salvation, a greater desire to know and serve God. During the past several decades, renewal has often been tethered more precisely to the involvement of the Holy Spirit in bringing spiritual refreshment. Attention has thus focused upon the reality of his presence and power available to believers, the use of his gifts among them, and the growth of Christ-like fruit within them. Yet certain pain seems always to reside along with the pleasures of renewal. People become uncomfortable. Cliques develop. Sometimes this happens consciously as some folks "come apart and become separate" from those they consider being still spiritually unenlightened. Others purposely draw apart from those who have, in their opinion, become fanatics and have departed from their denominational traditions. At other times, there is an unconscious regrouping into spiritually compatible comfort zones without a specific rationale for doing so.

As cliques informally develop, organizational groups follow similar lines. Prayer groups separate the "hot" Christians from the "lukewarm" or "cold" ones. Fellowship meetings are attended on the basis of whether they are the kind people have been used to or whether they offer new freedom of expression in song, prayer and body movements. Congregations within congregations form as different hours of worship use varied formats for the service. One becomes the pipe organ congregation, while the other becomes the guitar congregation. Sometimes, the division is made on the basis of what you do with your hands.. at one you sit with hands folded in reverence, while at the other you raise your hands in praise.

Renewal connected to the Holy Spirit is like Babel revisited. People who spoke one language together start having difficulty understanding each other. There is a new language called "speaking in tongues." Worse than Babel, no one claims to be able to understand most of it. Suddenly there is a new respect and reverence for something billed as experiential, yet unintelligible. Vocabulary also changes. "Gifts," "spirit- baptism," "filled," "the Lord spoke to me" are only some of the terms that cause excitement in some people and confusion in others.

Congregational pain is felt as a split develops among the membership. It may be a split in loyalty. Part of the congregation revels in the signs of new spiritual life, while others are saddened and see them as a strategy of Satan to destroy the church. It might be that the split centers on allegiance to, or rebellion against, the spiritual leader or some other pivotal person in the congregation. What begins as only a split of loyalty within a congregation can lead to a split in fact, where one of the factions physically disconnects from the other. It may be that division stops short of group action and there are only individual members who are called out, kicked out, or frozen out.

Such congregational pain may also show itself in plans

and purposes being changed or challenged. Prayer groups begin to dot the church calendar. Plain old get-together type of fellowship is questioned and greater spiritual depth or "sharing" is demanded of such occasions. A variety of worship expressions challenge and even shatter the familiar ones of the past. Conversations seem to elevate whatever is "spiritual" and downgrade what is labeled only "worldly."

PASTORS EXPERIENCE PAIN

The Holy Spirit is a pain. *Pastors have felt the pain.*

"Renewed by the Spirit," a pastor becomes suspect by the old guard in the congregation. They always thought he was a dependable leader. Now they are not so sure. At the same time, he becomes spotlighted by those with similar renewal experiences. In their enthusiastic endorsement, he receives publicity and accolades that are not necessarily helpful to him.

He may well be put on informal probation by his peers and church leadership. Pastoral fellowship develops strains and stresses similar to what is going on in the congregation. Pastors are as capable of forming cliques among themselves as is the general membership. A pastor who espouses a new brand of renewal may be labeled a problem, and , unconsciously or literally, may be placed on an unwanted list. He may even be in danger of being removed from his denominational clergy roster.

Not all the pain is externally caused. A pastor may become a martyr in his own mind and even solicit persecution as evidence that he stands in the center of God's will (therefore the world hates him). A search for a new ministry may begin. This can be a result of an authentic call of the Lord. However, it may be only a fad that develops when spiritual renewal strikes.

Meanwhile, the pastor without any new or different spiritual experience also feels pain. He becomes threatened by his peers or those in his congregation who testify to new life in Christ. After all, he is the spiritual leader and should be at the forefront of any move of God. To be breathing the dust of others who seem to be spiritually outpacing him is not a comfortable sensation.

Neither is it comfortable to have his theology or lifestyle challenged. Both become suspect and targets, especially on the part of the spiritually renewed ones whose zeal outruns their maturity.

Called to be pastor of one flock, the appearance of separated little flocks within the larger one is problematic. Torn between camps of religious "haves" and "have nots," a pastor yearns for some middle ground from which all his members will be reachable.

Additional pain results from an intensified critique of his preaching and teaching. His study and style may not have changed, but now there is criticism that he is not fiery enough or that he is not giving adequate "food" to those with an increased appetite for the Word of God.

INDIVIDUAL MEMBERS EXPERIENCE PAIN

The Holy Spirit is a pain. *The pain has been felt by individual members.*

There is an uncertainty as to what is going on. Those who are on new spiritual ground have a mix of excitement and apprehension. They feel they now have a greater inner sensitivity toward the Lord, but they do not have a point of reference. Not many in the congregation share their experiences. Doubts assail them from without, instigated by other members or even their pastor, and from within through times of inner restlessness. Some have been given the false impression that now everything in life will come up roses. When the thorns reappear, they question the validity of their own renewal experience.

Those who are without any recent, drastic or dramatic encounter with the Spirit also feel the pain of uncertainty. At times it is hidden under a harsh criticism of the "fanatics" in their midst. At other times, a silent judgment turns inward as they feel convicted for having such a routine Christian experience. They may even become very envious of those who have new spiritual dimensions in their lives.

Some of the individual pain is like that of a sheep in a wilderness without a shepherd close at hand. Many people have been introduced to unfamiliar gifts or manifestations of the Spirit while away from home, or at least away from the confines of their own congregations. They may have traveled to hear a speaker holding meetings in another town. They may have been invited by friends in another denomination. They may have been ministered to by a traveling evangelist who soon leaves town and goes to his next engagement. He only shares their momentary spiritual high and is not around for questions, conversation, or counseling when the lowlands of the everyday must be traversed.

Individual pain is felt in the circle of family and friends too. Suddenly a new awkwardness is encountered. Distance replaces closeness as people are no longer so sure of each other. Conversations are more guarded. There is trouble identifying with each other. There is some question about others being able to understand any more. What still holds from their past together? What doesn't? Now one person has "gotten so religious you can't talk together any more." Or the one with new spiritual experiences feels that even close family members won't comprehend what has taken place.. or don't care to.

FAULTY DIAGNOSIS?

All of the pain cited thus far is real. But often *a misdiagnosis has been made regarding the pain.* Pain is not always bad. Yet in many conclusions drawn about the Holy Spirit, pain has automatically invited negative judgment.

In congregations, strife, division, and people getting uncomfortable with one another are judged as something that should not be. Therefore, the cause (interest in the work and ministry of the Holy Spirit) is condemned. But pain is often good and necessary. It helps you focus on something that needs attention. Would you like to have a decay in your tooth go unnoticed until the tooth is ready to fall out of your mouth? Or would you rather have a toothache alert you to the need of having your dentist locate and treat the bad tooth? A little pain would contribute toward saving the tooth for many good years of chewing!

Pain can serve good purposes in a congregation. Pain can draw attention to matters that should be allowed to surface and be dealt with. In fact, most every denomination has its roots in this kind of pain. Usually a teaching or practice was being neglected. Pain accompanied the procedure of focusing attention on the issues. A new denomination was born in the wrenching apart that took place as some left their old fellowship and began trumpeting long-forgotten sounds. In the Lutheran Reformation, those sounds were "Scripture alone, Grace alone, Faith alone." Most denominations can tell of their birth by citing the pains experienced in those historic moments.

In congregations, things can become too routine and comfortable. There can be so much control exerted that change, even for the better, is taboo. There can be a dire lack of creativity. There can be real need for newness and freshness. Things can be so carefully programmed that there is little openness to the Lord's direction. Instead of being pliable and available for shaping by the Lord, congregations may become hardened into molds that leave no room for imaginative ministry. Worship can become more stifling than stimulating. Bible study can be ho hum, and schedules appear the same year after year on the church activity calendar. One pastor tells of a church secretary reading the minutes at an annual meeting. She got mixed up and read the minutes from *two* years back. No one caught the error because things were done in the same way no matter what year it was!

Even church facilities may remain unchanged, out of respect for the original building committee. People who become alert to current needs may promote new buildings or alterations to the old. Members of the initial building program may take such suggestions as judgment for not having done an adequate job, instead of rejoicing that younger and different people are now exerting leadership. Such a congregation and community need the benefit of fresh, inflicted pain to spur improvement. Additional prayer groups or home study groups now appear on the church calendar. A certain pain may be felt by the pastor and small group who have always and only met at the Wednesday night midweek study. Yet multiplication of physical cells is a sign of life, so why not take multiplication of cell groups within a congregation as also a sign of spiritual life?

If worship is "worth-ship," and if some people in the congregation have grown in their awareness of how worthy God is to be praised, then it is a nice problem having to accommodate them with new opportunities for expression. New expressions may be jarring, painfully jarring, to some traditionalists. But they may well need to expand their appreciation for variety in the Body. It also needs to be said that those who now want to clap and shout need to grow in acknowledging the worth of some of the changeless expressions of worship that connect us to Christians of long ago. For about three years, I rode the crest of new forms of worship. No two services were alike. I wrote new orders of worship, retranslated old ones, borrowed many I came across. (I wonder if those who criticized this knew how much extra work it required, and how much easier it would have been to always "Turn to page 57.") Nevertheless, I had to return to more traditional ways simply to acknowledge that the Spirit was not dependent upon my originality. He could indeed also bless people as they turned to page 57!

Making only a negative judgment upon the introduction of pain into congregational experience may well be quenching the Spirit and some very significant work he is seeking to do within that fellowship.

Pastors can profit by pain too. There are discomforts associated with spiritual growing as there are with physical growing. We found that "growing pains" are real as a doctor once explained the leg pains one of our sons was having. Likewise, a pastor necessarily feels pain that may be associated with his own spiritual development or that of the body of his congregation.

A pastor may feel uncomfortable with the renewal experience of a parishioner. He has prayed for that in his private and public prayers. Still, when it happens, he may not know what to do with it. This same dilemma has been experienced by spiritual leadership at all levels of the church. One response may be to secretly pray that renewal vanish as mysteriously as it appeared! Another may be to hope that, given some time, there will be an erosion of spiritual zeal, a return to "normalcy," and a recovery of a more manageable routine. Yet another response may be to oppose such renewal and show that heart and life were never in the lip-prayers made for increased spiritual vigor among the members.

The church cannot survive if the goal is to keep its leadership comfortable. There are plenty areas where pastors need compassionate understanding. However, to remove from them the discomfort of having to deal with spiritual renewal would be to make them and the people under their care less effective instruments of the Lord. While spiritual leaders counsel the necessity of confrontation when dealing with marital or other societal discord, this same counsel is often not applied in their own arenas. Avoidance, rather than confrontation, is too often practiced. New prayer groups may form, but the pastor has no contact with them. 20,000 may gather in a huge conference, and church leaders act as though nothing is going on. Distance might seem to offer the most comfort, but the pain of confrontation, or at least contact, will bear more fruit for the church. It will also be more in line with the example of Jesus who never avoided pain and discomfort to make it easier on himself. It also needs to be said that some pastors have honestly tried to be available and approachable and have been ignored, rebuffed, or even nearly crucified. Opening yourself to such discomfort doesn't guarantee success, but it does guarantee an approving smile from the Lord.

There is a discomfort associated with being surrounded by people who have experiences unlike your own, but then a pastor deals with this phenomenon every Sunday. He (one person) preaches a sermon (one message) to a whole roomful of people. The effect is varied. One listener is attentive; another is bored. One is greatly helped; another is incensed. One thinks a passage was well explained; another wonders how the pastor ever got those ideas from the text! Yet there is a mysterious and marvelous way that everyone gets something to apply to his or her particular life. The pastor will not be surprised, but rather heartened, if each one tells him at the door "Your message was helpful to me today."

If this can happen in the pew as the word is preached, why should it be surprising if the Spirit continues to minister uniquely to each one during the week between those worship services? While we marvel at God's creativity with snowflake and leaf, we fail to celebrate that same creativity in people's spiritual experiences. We should celebrate that too, and not castigate it. Until we learn such celebration, there is a need for discomfort and pain to nudge us toward the party. Otherwise we become like the pouting elder brother who refuses to join the fun and slinks away under the guise of some holy, sour responsibility.

Pastors can be uncomfortable with the surfacing of new texts from Scripture. Pericopes (the assigned readings for each Sunday) are an encouragement toward a varied exposure to Scripture. But they can be a prison. They often deal with bits and pieces from scattered sources. They are chosen to mesh rather than collide with one another on a given Sunday. They can be used as much to avoid dealing with difficult subjects as they can be a discipline, at other times, to deal exactly with them. They pass over topics lightly and go on to another next Sunday. But in charismatic renewal, people settle down in 1st Cor. 12-14 and tend to file a homestead. This concentrates attention on verses long neglected, quickly brushed aside, not taken seriously, or even crossed out. John 3:16 ("God so loved..") is easier to deal with than is 1st Corinthians 14:5 ("Now I want you all to speak in tongues.."). But, as the hymn writer puts it, "God's word is like a deep, deep mine," and what we find there are jewels not of our own making or design. A miner could tell us better about the discomforts and rewards of this labor. There is a claustrophobia involved in entering more narrow, restricted passages of Scripture. But the same Lord who has hidden diamonds in the bowels of the earth has placed treasure in some of the more obscure niches of his word. An invitation to dig should not be avoided. Those who sit outside and above the mine don't share the joy of discovering the jewels.

There is a pain associated with the destruction of stereotypes. When I became more open to charismatic concerns, many of my pastor friends assumed I no longer valued the Sacraments. They were disbelieving when I told them that my baptism as an infant was more precious to me than it had ever been. The fact that I led my congregation into having the Sacrament of Holy Communion at every Sunday morning worship instead of only on the first Sunday confused those who thought that renewal always destroys traditional values.

I have had to deal with stereotypes of my own. I have always had a suspicion that dramatic conversions are temporary in their effects. I remember how impressed I was to find that the couple who were volunteer youth leaders in my wife's home congregation had been doing that for many years, ever since their conversion at a Billy Graham Crusade. When a rather stylish couple in my congregation were converted, they came to me for some useful assignment in the church. I hid my surprise, arranged for them to visit patients at the hospital on Saturdays, and wondered how long that would last. When I left the congregation 12 years later, they were still at it!

One year, I had my young confirmands act out some of the events of the Passion week. This included footwashing. They agreed that it was easier to wash someone else's feet than to have their own feet washed. It is the same with forgiveness. It is easier to forgive (and admit someone else was wrong) than to be forgiven (admit your own wrong). When you jettison a long-held stereotype, there is the pain of admitting you were in error. The freedom is well worth the pain, however.

Pain is a spiritual necessity in the growth of individual members also. Renewal brings a need for painful assessment of goals and evaluation of life. Motivations are examined, and new courses are charted. Sharing and sacrifice replace hoarding and self-concern. The pain of Abraham's willing sacrifice of Isaac is better understood through the pain of laying lesser but real, long-held treasures upon the altar. Taking a servant role in a cause may replace only giving some money to it, but not without struggle and anguish. There is also discomfort that accompanies holding new convictions, and having to uphold them under scrutiny of family, friends, and business associates.

Patience exerts its own kind of pain, and there is great call for patience. Certainly patience is required as young or new "on-fire" Christians pass through their "know-it-all/do-it-all" phase. There seems to be an adolescent stage that follows spiritual rebirth. It is a passing thing (hopefully) on the way to maturity, but it can be a painful passage for everyone around.

The individual who experiences renewal needs to practice patience, even though painful, toward many. There is the old fellowship at church. It hasn't known the dramatic turn-around of the individual. Its routine hasn't changed much. There is the old association with family and friends. If the Lord took 30-40 years in dealing with you, don't expect instant turnarounds on the part of others.

There is also the same pastor at the church. One man told this amusing story:

"Remember how Moses was sitting at his desk in Pharaoh's palace? One day the Lord said to him, 'Moses, I would like to use you to lead your people out of Egypt.' Moses replied, 'I think I can handle that without too much trouble,' and he proceeded to go out and kill an Egyptian!

"God said, 'Moses, I think we need a little time together before you are ready!'

"Well, our group had been to a revival. We came back to our church and proceeded to kill the pastor. He didn't understand and appreciate our enlightenment. He didn't preach deep and exciting sermons.

"All the while that we were cutting our pastor to pieces, a little old lady kept telling us we must not do that to our Shepherd. We must pray for him instead.

"For a long time, we didn't listen to her. Finally we heard her soft voice, and we began to pray for our pastor.

"The results were amazing! His rapid spiritual growth surprised us. His preaching now had something for all of us! Had he changed? Or had we?"

Lacking patience, people unhitch from basic pictures

painted in Scripture. For example, the sheep may desire to roam where they think there are greener pastures. They forget that it is the shepherd, not the sheep, who rightfully chooses the grazing ground! Another example relates to the frequent complaint that "I am not being properly fed." Such complaint forgets the servant concept in Scripture. The picture in the New Testament is that of a slave, "doulos." A slave never had the luxury of complaining about the food. He wasn't there to eat it. He only carried the food to others. The servant question is not "Am I being properly fed?" The good servant asks "Is there a way I can better serve food to others?" Revived Christians need to be reminded about asking the right questions, painful though they be.

The ultimate target of our impatience is God himself. How presumptuous we sometimes become. We can't understand why God doesn't have as clear a picture of the situation as we do. His action (or inaction) seems inappropriate. His timing could certainly be improved upon! Finally and painfully we learn that his sovereign will just isn't enhanced by our attempted intrusions and alterations.

GOOD AND PAINFUL

The Holy Spirit is not the pain he is often written off as being. He is not a pain without purpose or only for negative reasons and results. He uses pain for good and in order to be helpful. Through it, he alerts us to needs ("Where does it hurt?" is more than a curious question by a good Doctor). Through pain, the Holy Spirit shapes and molds his people (Think of what clay and marble could tell us if they could sense and interpret to us the pain they feel at the hands of an artist). Through pain, the Holy Spirit increases our wisdom (No archaeologists or members of a dig escape pain in their quest for wisdom and knowledge).

The Holy Spirit, as Comforter and Counselor, has to deal with the reality of people and situations, not fake circumstances, in order to be helpful. The exercise of the gifts of the Holy Spirit (1st Cor. 12) can be painful, but they are for the common good. The exercise of the fruits of the Holy Spirit

(Gal. 5) can be painful because they are against the natural tendency of the flesh, but they hold the promise of great blessing to others.

The Holy Spirit... a bird? In a way, but not for clipping of wings or for caging. Rather, for assurance of presence, for peace, for freedom.

The Holy Spirit... a pain? In a way, but not for injury, insult, or trouble. Rather, for shaping, for alertness to needs, for growth, for maturity.

"It's a bird!"... "It's a pain!"... Not really.

More properly, "He's the Holy Spirit!"

* * *

Note the "Think/Talk/Pray about" section relating to Chapter 2.

CHAPTER THREE

*T*he Holy Spirit in the Life of Jesus

Have you ever thought of the Trinity as being composed of two friends and a stranger? The Father and the Son are the friends; the Holy Spirit is the stranger. The old adage says "Two is company, three is a crowd." Many Christians are comfortable in the company of the Father and Son, but they begin to feel a bit crowded with the Holy Spirit's presence on the scene. Though this may be overstating the case a bit, it is nevertheless true and tragic that the one who is called by such intimate names as "Comforter" and "Counselor" is sometimes unacknowledged and often misunderstood.

He is on the first page of the Bible..."and the Spirit of God was moving over the face of the waters" (Gen. 1:2). He is on the very last page of Scripture... "The Spirit and the Bride say, 'Come'" (Rev. 22:17). Over half of the Old Testament books make reference to him. Isaiah is as Spirit-centered as the book of Acts. It is Isaiah's writing that contains the beautiful Spirit-connected prophecies of Jesus. "There shall come forth a shoot from the stump of Jesse, and a branch shall grow out of his roots. And the Spirit of the Lord shall rest upon him, the spirit of wisdom and understanding, the spirit of counsel and might, the spirit of knowledge and the fear of the Lord" (Isaiah 11:1-2).

The Holy Spirit's involvement in the life and ministry of Jesus is the best example of how necessary is the participation of the Holy Spirit in the spiritual health and growth of all

Christians. A survey will show the empowerment and encouragement which came to Jesus through the presence of the Spirit of God.

PRE-CONCEPTION EVENTS

John the Baptist was involved as a prelude to Jesus long before John began preaching in the wilderness. In fact, the announcement of John's coming birth created quite a stir in Jerusalem. Many people were there when Zechariah went to burn the incense in the temple (Luke 1:10). Gabriel's appearance to Zechariah caused him to be in the temple longer than usual. The crowd began wondering about that. They wondered even more when he came out, unable to speak a word. Perhaps the crowd never did find out what had happened until John was born and his father could speak again, about six months before Jesus' birth.

Zechariah hadn't believed the angel when told that Elizabeth would bear him a child. Similar news had given Abraham and Sarah a good laugh years ago (Gen. 17:17, 18:12). Though Zechariah hadn't laughed, his disbelief brought him a sentence of silence until John's birth. Part of what he would be left to only ponder was the angel's message that this child to be born would be "filled with the Holy Spirit, even from his mother's womb" (Luke 1:15). As though out of his own astonishment, Luke twice repeats the fact that John "leaped for joy" in Elizabeth's womb when Mary first came to share the news of her own conception. While the Holy Spirit literally moved John in the womb, he also moved Elizabeth to her outburst of blessing upon Mary's arrival (Luke 1:42-45). When John was born, Zechariah's voice returned and he was promptly filled with the Holy Spirit and given words of prophecy about his newborn son (Luke 1:67-79).

CONCEPTION

Palestine buzzed with the news that old Zechariah and Elizabeth were about to have a son. That would ordinarily be a hard act to follow. But the next number on the program was a birth to take place without benefit of a husband's participation at all! Matthew begins his account with the sentence, "Now the birth of Jesus Christ took place in this way" (Matt. 1:18). Many of the following events invite the quizzical response.."You're not serious! You've got to be kidding!" Joseph's response was quite close to this. A "Very Revised Version" might have him say "Conceived by the Holy Spirit? Spirit! Schmirit! I'll give you a quiet divorce, that's what I'll do. The business with Elizabeth and Zechariah is enough already. But this, Mary, is too much!"

The Holy Spirit is a great convincer, however. Soon Joseph accepted the strange events as truth (Matt. 1:20), and the rest of his life proved how powerfully convicted he was about the God- connectedness of all this. Although it is not all recorded, he paid for his convictions by enduring all the ridicule and smart remarks that surely were leveled at him, his wife, and child. He paid with the obvious loss of business due to his absence from his carpentry shop, and he paid with the hardships he experienced as he protected and provided for his family on that extended trip to Egypt.

BIRTH

So often, the Virgin birth is understood to be God shouting only "Hey, my Son is Divine!" It did that, but God was shouting even more loudly, "Hey, my son is human!" It was an incredible step down for Jesus. He really let go of his equality with God, came in the flesh, and dealt with life on the same terms as we must. He also limited himself to using the same equipment available to people. He didn't keep his divinity in his back pocket, like some awesome credit card to be drawn out and used if he got in a bind. He gave all that up and used instead whatever accrued to him as a son in proper relationship with the heavenly Father. Everything about his time on earth would be reduced to masquerade if this were not true. The secret of his love, his wisdom, his faithfulness to his mission, his power against his foes, his ultimate victory was his appropriation of all that the Holy Spirit of God made available to him. Jesus' Spirit-connection, having begun at his conception and birth, was never broken.

PRESENTATION

Old man Simeon could have taught us much about the Holy Spirit. Three verses of introduction in Luke (2:25-27) tell three Spirit-related things about Simeon. The Holy Spirit was upon him; it is made to sound like a continuous abiding, rather than an on- again, off-again thing. Secondly, the Holy Spirit had revealed to him that he would not die until he had seen the Lord's Christ. Thirdly, he was inspired by the Spirit to go to the temple at the exact same time that Mary and Joseph came, bringing Jesus with them, for the performance of all that the law required.

It was no accident that the prophetess Anna also joined the scene. She must have been as Spirit-directed as Simeon. Her words about the redemption of Jerusalem confirmed the witness that Simeon had made about Jesus (Luke 2:38).

GROWTH IN WISDOM

That the boy Jesus grew in wisdom is documented by the gospel writer Luke in a way that forms brackets around Jesus' visit to the temple at age twelve. First it is reported that Jesus spent his childhood in Nazareth where he "grew and became strong, filled with wisdom; and the favor of God was upon him" (Luke 2:40). Then comes the account of Jesus' trip with his parents to Jerusalem. His perplexed parents lost four days of travel before locating their son in the temple. But there he was, naturally sharing a sample of the God-given wisdom that was his. We should note that evidence of his wisdom was not only in what he said; it also was shown in how he listened and in the kinds of questions he asked (Luke 2:46-47).

Nearly twenty years are then wrapped up by Luke in the words, "And Jesus increased in wisdom and in stature, and in favor with God and man" (Luke 2:52). So wisdom is the first gift of the Spirit attributed to Jesus. Perhaps this is why St. Paul lists wisdom first when he mentions a variety of gifts in 1st Corinthians 12.

BAPTISM

Luke doesn't make as much of Jesus' baptism as do some of the other gospel writers. Matthew indicates that John the Baptist almost got into an argument with his cousin when Jesus came to be baptized. John thought that he was not the one to be baptizing the Messiah. If anything, the Messiah should be baptizing him (Matt. 3:14). St. John devotes a good share of his first chapter to events surrounding Jesus' baptism. Luke, however, is rather nonchalant about it. "Now when all the people were baptized, and Jesus also had been baptized.." (Luke 3:21). I think that Jesus would have liked that way of reporting it. He had requested baptism in order to identify himself with the rest of the people. He never took any shortcuts just because he was the Son of God. He was God in the flesh, and he went the way of all flesh. Baptism was only the beginning. You know from the rest of the story that he didn't take shortcuts even when the way of all flesh meant suffering, and dying, and entering the tomb.

Jesus needed the assurance that God was with him. Remember his torment on the cross when the sins of the world pressed upon him and he cried "My God, my God, why hast thou forsaken me?" (Mark 15:34). How different it was at his baptism! The dove came down as a visible sign of accompaniment by the Holy Spirit, and the voice from heaven told Jesus what he needed to hear. "Thou art my beloved son; with thee I am well pleased" (Luke 3:22).

Baptism took on an added cargo of meaning from that time. Prior to that, it had been a rather gruesome event. It was a baptism unto repentance, accompanied by much sadness, confession of sin, wailing, sackcloth and ashes. From the time of Jesus' baptism, however, it became a celebration of relationship, a celebration of life and life in the Spirit.

Do you know your baptismal date? If you don't, find it out. The anniversary of your baptism is cause for celebration.

Birthdays are a reason to celebrate "I have been given life *by* God!" Baptisms are a reason to celebrate "I have been given life *with* God!" Your baptism is not only an historic act which took place in the dim past. It is a live option. Don't place false hope on some long-forgotten act, but do place proper emphasis on your present relationship with God which began in that act. Event alone becomes history; relationship is current event.

Do you assuredly hear God speaking the same message to you as he did to Jesus? "You are my beloved son, my beloved daughter, my dear child; with you I am well pleased." God can say that about you because Jesus did everything for you to make you pleasing in God's sight. He took your sins upon himself so that the Father can look at you as though you are his perfect son or daughter. The Apostle Paul says that baptism identifies you with Jesus' sacrifice and victory. "Do you not know that all of us who have been baptized into Christ Jesus were baptized into his death? We were buried therefore with him by baptism into death, so that as Christ was raised from the dead by the glory of the Father, we too might walk in newness of life" (Romans 6:3-4). That newness includes new status as part of God's family, members of his kingdom and heirs to eternity. The initiation to all this was our baptism.

I have personally made confession of Jesus as my Lord and Savior, but if you want a date for my time of being born again, I'll give you my baptismal date. I like the term "born again" but I don't like that so many speak of it as though they gave themselves birth by their own believing. *Life is given to you by an action not your own.* That's true physically, unless you presume to have arranged your own birth! Life is given to you by an action not your own. That is also true in a spiritual sense. If I had absolutely no other reason to baptize infants, I would do so because it is the best witness of how God receives us without any performance on our part to make us worthy. Infant baptism is a great testimony to the truth of salvation by grace alone. Yet we must keep in mind that the major action in baptism is that of establishing relationship. Without a continuing and a growth in this relationship with the Lord, the purpose of baptism is frustrated.

Some translations record the voice from heaven as saying "Today I have begotten thee." Sounds like Jesus was also twice- born, doesn't it? I have it in my will that my baptismal date shall be inscribed on my gravestone. Not just a birthdate and deathdate. A Christian has something else...a beginning date that has no cutoff. By God's grace, my life with him had a start. By God's grace, my life with him has no ending. If this is also your confession, say Amen!

The Holy Spirit was an instrument in Jesus' baptism. He shares a role in every baptism that takes place with water and "In the name of the Father, Son and Holy Spirit." But there was another way in which Jesus would use the Holy Spirit as *content* and not only as agent. Not one of the gospel writers neglects stating that Jesus would baptize with the Holy Spirit (Matthew and Luke also add "and with fire"). We will pursue the meaning of this ongoing kind of baptism in succeeding chapters.

TEMPTATION

In Nehemiah, chapter 9, Ezra summarizes God's dealings with the Children of Israel. They had been instructed by the Spirit (vs. 20), and had not lacked food, water or clothes for forty years. They possessed the promised land and experienced power and plenty. "They captured fortified cities and a rich land, and took possession of houses full of good things, cisterns hewn out, vineyards, olive orchards and fruit trees in abundance; so they ate, and were filled and became fat, and delighted themselves in thy great goodness" (vs. 25). But they became presumptuous, forgot the word of the Lord, and fell again and again into the hands of their enemies.

Compare this with the temptation of Jesus. He too was "full of the Spirit" and "was led by the Spirit for forty days in the wilderness, tempted by the devil" (Luke 4:1-2). In his wilderness experience of forty days, he went without food. No manna appeared to sustain him, yet he turned down easy promises of bread and power. He refused to act presumptuously and still expect God's automatic protection. Homes, vineyards and cisterns had suddenly come into the hands of the Israelites after their forty years of wandering. After his time in the wilderness, Jesus refused the temptation to pick up stone and have it turn into bread, even though he was hungry. The Israelites had marvelous victory over their enemies, and extended the borders of their earthly kingdom. Jesus refused that kind of worldly power. With everything going for them, the Israelites soon wandered from God, but still presumed that his blessing would accompany them. With nothing going for him, Jesus refused to force God's protective hand by jumping off a high pinnacle of the temple.

Bereft of all but the Spirit's presence and the wisdom of the written word, Jesus stood the test despite the lack of many positives that the Israelites had been given. Theirs was to be a mission of blessing to the world but it was frustrated by their own disobedience. Jesus' greater victory over the devil set the scene for his greater mission of blessing to the world. Jesus knew, as did Elihu, that his life-cord was the Holy Spirit. "The spirit of God has made me, and the breath of the almighty gives me life" (Job 33:4). He never sought to be independent of this source of strength and guidance.

MINISTRY

A great heresy in the church is the denial of Jesus' humanity. Outside the church there may be a denial of his divinity; within the church his divinity is accepted, though used against him. For example, Jesus tells us to "Love one another as I have loved you" (John 15:12). It is tempting for us to respond, "Well, Lord, we would *like* to, but after all, you were divine and we are only human!" So we do not take him seriously. We use a reverent reference to his divinity to get us off the hook of commitment. We really deny his humanity and act as though he is asking something that is beyond us. But he has never treated us that way. We *can*, in fact, love as he loved, if we appropriate the same loving and empowering presence of the Holy Spirit which Jesus did. Our faith is not in some little man who wasn't there. He *was* there, in the flesh, to break open all the options available to us in the flesh and to issue those higher callings, such as the one to love as he has loved.

After he had been tempted, he returned "in the power of the Spirit" to begin his ministry (Luke 4). He went to Nazareth, entered the synagogue, opened the book of Isaiah, and found where he was described in prophetic reference. "The Spirit of the Lord is upon me, because he has anointed me to preach good news to the poor. He has sent me to proclaim release to the captives and recovering of sight to the blind, to set at liberty those who are oppressed, to proclaim the acceptable year of the Lord" (Isaiah 61).

The people of his city would not accept that such a passage could find fulfillment in someone from the family of a local carpenter. So those folk took this not-so-favorite son out to a cliff where their plans to kill him were frustrated by unexplained circumstance. Perhaps the Spirit's power shield around Jesus prevented them from grabbing him as he walked out of their midst (Luke 4:30). Little did they know that this carpenter's son would soon encourage all who followed him to recognize that same Spirit-anointing, to accept the same mission of bringing good news, proclaiming release, opening eyes, and to stress "now" as the appropriate and acceptable time to recognize the sovereign lordship of God.

His hometown reception was typical of much of the suspicion with which he would have to deal. The greatest charge against him was that he operated as a tool of Satan. His answer was Spirit- related. "But if it is by the Spirit of God that I cast out demons, then the kingdom of God has come upon you" (Matt. 12:28).

Peter witnessed to Jesus' Spirit-empowered ministry as he told Cornelius "how God anointed Jesus of Nazareth with the Holy Spirit and with power; how he went about doing good and healing all that were oppressed by the devil, for God was with him" (Acts 10:38). Doing good exhibited the Spirit's fruit of love, healing was a gift of the Spirit, and so was the ability to discern who were the ones possessed by demons or oppressed by Satan.

TEACHING

When Nicodemus came to Jesus in need of some basic spiritual instruction, Jesus began with a short course on the Holy Spirit. Jesus acknowledged God's Spirit to be the source of all his teaching. "For the one whom God has sent speaks the words of God; to him God gives the Spirit without limit" (John 3:34, NIV).

When Jesus compared God the Father with the ability and willingness of earthly fathers to give gifts, he cited the Spirit as the highest gift God is most eager to bestow. "What father among you, if his son asks for a fish, will instead of a fish give him a serpent; or if he asks for an egg, will give him a scorpion? If you then, who are evil, know how to give good gifts to your children, how much more will the heavenly Father give the Holy Spirit to those who ask him!" (Luke 11:11-13).

Jesus encouraged his disciples to be confident should they ever have to testify to their faith in front of hostile people. "When they deliver you up, do not be anxious how you are to speak or what you are to say; for what you are to say will be given to you in that hour; for it is not you who speak, but the Spirit of your Father speaking through you" (Matt. 10:19-20). He followed his own teaching when he was later dragged before religious and governmental leaders who examined and accused him.

Sometimes he taught about the Holy Spirit in a way that would only later be understood by his disciples. St. John records that "On the last day of the feast, the great day, Jesus stood up and proclaimed, 'If any one thirst, let him come to me and drink. He who believes in me, as the scripture has said, Out of his heart shall flow rivers of living water'" (John 7:37-38). Then John adds this explanation: "Now this he said about the Spirit, which those who believed in him were to receive; for as yet the Spirit had not been given, because Jesus was not yet glorified" (John 7:39).

RESURRECTION

Jesus testified that he could do nothing of his own accord or authority (John 5:19,30). This also applied to his resurrection. It was no independent "do-it-yourself" project. It was a "done-for-him" event. Even when Jesus spoke of having power to lay down his life and take it up again, he set it within the framework of a charge which he had from the Father (John 10:17- 18). He did not simply "rise"; he "was raised." St. Paul says this clearly in Romans 8:11. "If the *Spirit of him who raised* Jesus from the dead dwells in you, *he who raised* Christ Jesus from the dead will give life to your mortal bodies also *through his Spirit* which dwells in you." It was this resurrection activity of the Spirit that designated Jesus "Son of God in power" according to Paul's introduction to the book of Romans (1:4).

In his glorified state, Jesus began at once to use the Holy Spirit as his empowering agent to equip his disciples for their mission in the world. John records a kind of first installment on Pentecost that occurred the evening of Easter Sunday. "Jesus said to them again, 'Peace be with you. As the Father has sent me, even so I send you.' And when he had said this, he breathed on them, and said to them, 'Receive the Holy Spirit. If you forgive the sins of any, they are forgiven; if you retain the sins of any, they are retained'" (John 20:21-23). He knew that between Easter and the first Pentecost they would already require the ability to discern the need for forgiveness and exercise it as a cohesive power in that early Christian fellowship.

ASCENSION

It would be proper to quote much of John 14-16 at this point. The many references by Jesus in those chapters foreshadow his necessary departure from his disciples. A sample of his words are in John 16:7. "Nevertheless I tell you the truth: it is to your advantage that I go away, for if I do not go away, the Counselor will not come to you; but if I go, I will send him to you."

I once heard a missionary explain some advantage that has accrued because Jesus replaced himself with the Holy Spirit. The missionary said that had Jesus remained on earth and visited one village a day up to this present time, he would still have been to only half the villages in India alone! But through the power and presence of the Holy Spirit in the lives of believers, the whole world in every generation has the potential of being reached with the good news of Jesus.

CONTINUING PRESENCE

Jesus would never have left the world if it would have frustrated God's plan of redemption and love. As he was Immanuel, "God with us," while he was on the earth, so the Holy Spirit continues to be Immanuel, "God with us," in an ongoing way. Jesus proved on earth what wonders of love and mercy can take place through a Father-related, Spirit-connected life. His example is meant to encourage his church toward a mission of adventurous blessing in this world.

* * *

Note the "Think/Talk/Pray about" section relating to Chapter 3.

CHAPTER FOUR

The Holy Spirit in the Life of the Church...He Calls

SEE WHO FOUND ME!

The same Spirit who worked in and through Jesus is the One who is operative in all Christians. As Martin Luther has written in The Small Catechism:

"I believe that I cannot by my own understanding or effort believe in Jesus Christ my Lord, or come to him. But the Holy Spirit has called me through the Gospel..."

"I believe that I cannot believe." This strange confession makes good spiritual sense. St. Paul said the same thing: "No one can say 'Jesus is Lord' except by the Holy Spirit" (Romans 12:3b). When an adult comes to faith, the person seems to be front and center on the stage, bathed in the spotlight at this significant moment. The real scene, however, is shown when a curtain rises behind the individual to display all the ways in which God has taken the initiative to move toward the believer who all the while "seemed" to be moving toward God.

An anonymous poet of the 19th century expressed it well:

"I sought the Lord, and afterward I knew
He moved my soul to seek him, seeking me;
It was not I that found, O Savior true;
No, I was found of thee."
Service Book And Hymnal, 473

"See what I found!" is an understandable exclamation at the point of discovery. But a more correct Christian witness shouts, "See who found me!" This is not to say that a person is uninvolved in the process of faith. For instance, suppose the telephone rings. A relative is calling to tell of an illness in the family. You pick up the receiver and give attention to the words of the message. You ask questions and gain more information. There is still more response on your part. The situation may require the time and expense of a trip. You are very involved in the process once you answer the phone instead of letting it ring. Yet despite the involvement, all of your action did not cause the phone to ring in the first place. An action not your own initiated the chain of events that led to getting the message. In fact, an action not your own was instrumental in your being a part of that family in the first place.

CALLING THROUGH/CALLING TO

Jesus did not come to earth by the invitation of the world but by the initiation of the Father. All that Jesus said and did could have become a forgotten and irrelevant part of the past. It has been the Spirit's task to keep it from being that. He does his work by a two-fold process of "calling through" and "calling to." He continues his work by repeating this process.

Luther wraps up the "calling through" action by saying that the calling is done "through the Gospel." The basic good news may come through the reading of the Bible, the hearing of a sermon, a conversation with a friend, a circumstance that you experience. The basic content of the call, however, is the Gospel.

Then there is the "calling to." The Spirit is as unique in the attention he gives to tailoring the call to an individual as the Father and Son have been unique in the creative and redemptive attention they have given to each person. That call may come as the good news of hope in despair, comfort in distress, forgiveness in guilt, strength in weakness, courage in fear, company in loneliness.

"Calling through" relates to the *means* of the call. "Calling to" represents the *ends* of the call. But then, instead of the means becoming the ends, the ends become the means. That

is, the Spirit uses the called ones to become the calling ones...
and so the family of believers grows.

DISTRIBUTOR

The calling activity of the Holy Spirit is emphasized by
Jesus in chapters 14-16 of John's Gospel. In John 16:13-15
Jesus said, "When the Spirit of truth comes, he will guide you
into all the truth; for he will not speak on his own authority,
but whatever he hears he will speak, and he will declare to
you the things that are to come. He will glorify me, for he will
take what is mine and declare it to you. All that the Father has
is mine; therefore I said that he will take what is mine and
declare it to you."

Sometimes, people act as though they have to protect the
members of the Trinity from each other. There are those who
are afraid that the Son diverts attention from the Father.
Others fear that the Spirit will crowd the Son off the center
stage. But there is no such worry within the Trinity. There is
beautiful agreement and cooperation between Father, Son
and Spirit. This passage in John shows that. The Father is
Possessor. The Son is Inheritor. The Spirit is Distributor.

Jesus never claimed sole authority over or possession of
anything. He acknowledged the Father as the source of all he
was, all he did, and all he said. "Truly, truly I say to you, the
Son can do nothing of his own accord, but only what he sees
the Father doing; for whatever he does, that the Son does
likewise" (John 5:19). On the other hand, the Father withheld
nothing of his own from the Son. "For the Father loves the
Son, and shows him all that he himself is doing" (John 5:20).
Earthly fathers know the joy of sharing what they have with
their children and seeing it blossom in their lives. And have
you ever thought less of sons or daughters who openly and
honestly pay tribute to parents who have been good to them?

It is out of this exemplary relationship that the Spirit
draws the content of what he shares with believers. Jesus
indicates full confidence in the manner in which the Spirit
will go about his work. "He will glorify me," said Jesus (John
16:14). The Church is not to worry. There is no competition

in the Godhead. Instead of competition, there is a grand cooperation that needs to be noted by the Church, and copied.

TRUE COUNSELOR

"And I will pray the Father, and he will give you another Counselor, to be with you forever, even the Spirit of Truth, whom the world cannot receive, because it neither sees him nor knows him; you know him, for he dwells with you, and will be in you" (John 14:16-17).

I have always admired a professional person who is willing to refer clients to someone else for help. A doctor who sends me to a specialist pays himself a compliment. It is not a reflection of his own limitations as much as it is evidence of really caring for his patient. So it is with a lawyer who may know another attorney who has handled more cases similar to mine. As he puts me in contact with him, my trust in that lawyer and my respect for him increases, not diminishes.

When Jesus referred his followers to the care and supervision of the Holy Spirit, he was being supremely concerned for the ongoing welfare of the Church. The fact that Jesus chose such terms as Counselor and Comforter shows the confidence he had in the future guidance that would be available to his people through the Spirit. The disciples were quite shaken when Jesus spoke to them of his departure. Thomas and Philip (John 14) most quickly voiced their inner thoughts and questions, although all the disciples were likely sharing their apprehension. But we have a Lord who always anticipates our needs. Just as the Father planned our redemption before we were even born, so Jesus had arranged for a "forever-Counselor" to assure that his disciples would not be left desolate.

There are counselors who only listen, depending on that activity to meet needs by simply airing fears or guilts. Other counselors primarily ask questions, counting on the answers to problems being within the troubled person and only needing to come to the surface. Certainly, listening and asking relevant questions are valid counseling techniques.

The counseling of the Spirit is more direct. He has the truth that is necessary to make a difference in lives and situations.

It is not a generally recognized truth, however. The world is more accustomed to delusion. It may be the casual falsehood practiced in personal niceties. "Hi! How are you?" "I'm fine, thanks." I may not be fine, but I am not honest enough to tell you the truth, or I may not think you have the time or interest to hear the truth.

I was at a worship service once when the pastor prefaced the Prayer of the Church by telling the congregation about the condition or need of people for whom we would be praying. He said there might be others who should be included and asked the congregation to mention any persons he had forgotten.

Elizabeth's hand shot up in the air and she called out, "Hey, how about me?" Elizabeth is a little woman with a beautiful, childlike mind. Her presence in the congregation is a natural blessing. As she leaves the church, many people seated along the aisle get a hug because she is so authentically happy to see them. Her frequent hospitalizations have often placed her on the congregation's prayer list. This was her first Sunday at worship after spending several days in bed.

Elizabeth taught me some lessons that Sunday. If I had been as honest as she was, I would have raised my hand and requested prayer too. I wonder how many others in church that day were saying under their breath, "Hey, how about me?" The pastor didn't hear those unspoken sighs. Neither did the other worshippers. Still, they did not go unheard. God hears our silent pleas, but worship would be enriched by more shared expressions, following the example of a candid child named Elizabeth.

Casual delusion is practiced in society and church, and it makes us less acquainted with truth. Then there are the contrived delusions. Political "necessities" cause outright lies to be clothed in words carefully chosen to mislead. All kinds of motivations for personal gain cause truth to be chucked out and falsehood to be employed. Consequently, the Spirit of truth comes as a stranger to the world that cannot receive him "because it neither sees him nor knows him."

It is different as he comes to believers. The Holy Spirit recognizes himself. A mutual affinity has been created as the Spirit dwells in the believer and then comes to the believer in still another dimension. The disciples had at the time only experienced the one dimension of the Spirit dwelling *with* them. The other promised dimension was when he would be *in* them. The Post-Pentecost Christian knows the combined blessing of the Spirit's "with" and "within" presence. By the way, the Spirit recognizes himself not only within a believer, but between believers. Only recently, in a crowd of inmates at a prison, I spotted a young man whose relationship with Jesus showed in his eyes. He came to me after the meeting before I had a chance to locate him in the crowd. We agreed that the Holy Spirit had recognized himself as we saw each other!

TEACHER/REMINDER

"But the Counselor, the Holy Spirit, whom the Father will send in my name, he will teach you all things, and bring to your remembrance all that I have said to you" (John 14:26).

Christa McAuliffe, who lost her life in the 1986 explosion of the space shuttle "Challenger", described her occupation in these words: "I touch the future. I teach." Teachers are instrumental in opening the awareness of young people to the world around them. They are an impressive force in shaping interests, understanding, attitudes and morals. Many people would cite a favorite teacher as one who played into their choice of study or life work. Teachers do touch the future. They call students into adventures of inquiring, learning and doing.

Christa's words could be borrowed by the Holy Spirit in explaining his role in the church: "I touch the future. I teach." We will look more at this role in a future chapter. It is enough to note here the connection between teaching and calling. It is the flash of new truth across the mind that sets or changes direction in people's lives. The truth about Jesus has struck people while on paths of their own choosing, and has sent them on totally different journeys. This literally happened to the Apostle Paul on the road to Damascus, and in similar ways to Constantine, Augustine and Luther. Not everyone can cite such drastic turnaround experiences, but all Christians have their special moments of meaning when spiritual truth has affected their response to the Lord.

Recall, as well as call, is part of the Spirit's portfolio. He will "bring to remembrance all that I have said to you" (John 14:26). The Holy Spirit, not some high-tech corporation, offers us the best in personal computering services! A good dose of both assurance and motivation can be taken from this verse. Even though we may never be dragged before governors and kings (Matt. 10:18), the aid of the Spirit in the action of recall is reassuring. I am less and less impressed by coincidences in life and more and more convinced that they are "God-incidents." A person may be terribly depressed, worried, remorseful, or experiencing physical or mental anguish. At a significant moment, the person "happens" to remember something that eases the depression, replaces the worry, assures pardon, or gives strength necessary to endure. That is not coincidence. That is a God- incident, and proper credit should be given him. Often that "something" is a word of Scripture, a promise of God. The Holy Spirit is in the business of recall, of recollection of the good news at a good and helpful time. Robert Frost has written of taking "the road less traveled by, and that has made all the difference." Because so many are not responsive to the call and recall of the Spirit, the Christian's path is the narrow, less used one, but taking it makes all the difference.

Besides assurance, there is also motivation in these words of Jesus about the Spirit's recall activity. Even the Spirit cannot draw water from a dry well. Jesus' promise is not that the Spirit will manufacture a message that has never been known or accepted. Rather, the "bringing to remembrance" presupposes an unconscious reservoir, but a reservoir nevertheless. Consequently, there is great motivation for hearing, studying and storing up the content of Scripture in order to give the Spirit a biblical pool from which to draw.

I once heard an Air Force officer tell of his experience as

a prisoner of war. If a letter came, the guard would let the prisoner only open it and barely begin reading it. Then the guard would snatch it away. The torment of not being able to read the letter was nearly worse than not receiving it at all. His mother had the habit of incorporating Scripture verses in her letters. Since no Bibles were available, this was his only source of God's word. In the brief time he had before the guard retrieved the letter, he would skim the pages for the Bible passages. Then, as best he could, he would commit them to memory.

With free access to the Scripture, you and I need only the proper motivation and ordering of our time to give the Holy Spirit more spiritual fodder for his use and our welfare.

WITNESS BEARER/WITNESS MAKER

"But when the Counselor comes, whom I shall send to you from the Father, even the Spirit of truth, who proceeds from the Father, he will bear witness to me; and you also are witnesses, because you have been with me from the beginning" (John 15:26- 27).

It sounds like a scene in a Western Union office, doesn't it? The Father is the office manager, Jesus is the dispatcher, and the Holy Spirit is the carrier of the message. Once again, the cordial arrangement within the Trinity is apparent. The Holy Spirit willingly serves as runner on errands not his own. He bears the message of another and for another. He is a spotlight focusing on Jesus, and a searchlight seeking people. He is a witness bearer.

But in the very action of being a witness bearer, he is also a witness maker. The evidence used to call people to Christ is the same spiritual stuff that is the basis for Christian witness. Note that the word is "witnesses," not "salesmen." God's method of getting his word and work out into the world and to the attention of people is often misunderstood. In the minds of many, this appears to be the job for salespersons. The Apostles and disciples are thought to be the sales representatives, the Holy Spirit is the teacher/trainer, and Pentecost becomes the quickie course on salesmanship.

They get psyched up for selling Jesus, they hit the streets, and soon 3000 people are sold the whole package!

If you read the story of the early church in this frame of mind, you shake your head and say, "I'm not cut out for that. I believe in God and all, but when it comes to selling someone else on it, I'm no good. Some people are natural evangelists, but I'm not. I like to listen, and I can give some money, but I'm no salesman!" Thus, Christian evangelism is thought of as some kind of hard sell. The effective evangelist or congregation is the one most successful in an effective "close" where the "buyer" ends up repeating certain words or phrases that certify the sale.

I admire the talents of good sales personnel, but the idea of salesmanship has created confusion regarding the proclamation of Jesus. This confusion has effectively encouraged many Christians to keep their mouths shut and let evangelism be done by some corp of elite, polished salesmen. *This is not what Jesus had in mind.* He addresses anyone who acknowledges him as Lord and Savior, and he does not say "You are salespersons." He says, "You are witnesses." It is not optional. Jesus didn't ask "Will you be witnesses?" He did not command "You must be witnesses." The grammar he used states a simple, continuing fact: "You *are* witnesses."

If you see an accident on the corner, you are a witness. Whether you ever get questioned in court, you are still a witness to that accident. You may deny it, refuse to talk about it, but the fact remains that you are a witness. Being such a witness doesn't mean that you are responsible to "sell" the reporting officer regarding whose fault it was. You are not obligated to run to the courthouse and convince judge and jury to believe the details. On the other hand, your witness may be needed to bring about a just settlement or to keep an innocent party from suffering. No one would respect you for withholding your witness if that were the case, but no one would expect you to suddenly become a charming persuader or a forceful salesperson either... just a witness.

It would be a bit ridiculous if you said to the officer, "I'm afraid I am not cut out for this sort of thing. Get the lawyer down the street. He is a much better speaker." But *you* are the witness, and you have a unique perspective regarding the accident. Perhaps several people saw it happen. One could only see the front of the car, the other the rear. One saw the driver, while another witness saw the tire blow out. Each one had a particular view of the accident. Yours is unlike that of any other.

The same is true of your Christian witness. You have a unique perspective. God has touched your life with the love of Jesus in a way that is special. You alone are witness to it. If you withhold that witness, it will never be made, and some other lives will be poorer because of it.

CONVINCER

"And when he comes, he will convince the world of sin and of righteousness and of judgment; of sin, because they do not believe in me; of righteousness, because I go to the Father, and you will see me no more; of judgment, because the ruler of this world is judged" (John 16:8-11).

Whenever I worked as a salesman, I used my training, material and presentation in as convincing a manner as possible. I can be much more relaxed as a Christian witness, because I am not the convincer. The One who calls also convinces. Knowing that the Spirit accompanies any witness to Jesus gives a Christian a special kind of "cool." The Spirit is complimented as we relax and depend on his interest and his ability as a convincer. He is insulted if we rely on our own cleverness. Remember, the witness isn't responsible for convincing judge and jury. The defense or prosecution has that responsibility. You and I are not the convincers; we are witnesses. We are "evidence" that the Holy Spirit can use to convince others.

The Spirit's desire is to convince of sin, including the basic sin of unbelief, and to bring people to repentance. His goal is to convince of righteousness, the finished and Father-accepted salvation, and to offer forgiveness and grace. He aspires to convince of judgment, because Satan has been defeated, and to let people experience the fruit of victory. He finds no joy in convictions that only condemn.

ONGOING CALLING

We have dealt primarily with the more general and basic activity of the Holy Spirit as he calls to faith in Jesus through the Gospel. There are many biblical references to more specific and temporary "callings" of the Spirit. These are especially plentiful in the book of Acts. They deal with messages to proclaim, priorities to acknowledge, places to go. These ongoing nudges by the Spirit are described in a variety of ways:
- "And the Spirit said to Philip.." (8:29).
- "And the Spirit told me to go with them.." (11:12).
- "So being sent out by the Holy Spirit.." (13:4).
- "For it has seemed good to the Holy Spirit and to us.." (15:28).
- "..having been forbidden by the Holy Spirit to speak the word in Asia" (16:6).
- "..except that the Holy Spirit testifies to me in every city that imprisonment and afflictions await me" (20:23).
- "Through the Spirit they told Paul not to go to Jerusalem" (21:4).

There is no intention here to minimize the reality and significance of these ongoing calls. However, the day by day experience of the Spirit will be dealt with in a later chapter.

* * *

Note the "Think/Talk/Pray about" section relating to Chapter 4.

CHAPTER FIVE

*T*he Holy Spirit in the Life of the Church...He Gathers

A young Christian girl had just been laid off from work for the summer. She determined to devote her extra time to the reading of Christian books. Already she had finished six of them, probably surpassing the yearly average for most adults! She was such an eager and absorbent young person. When she spoke of conversations with other Christian people, she referred to them as "spiritual feasts." This had not always been the pattern of her life, but she now had an infectious desire to be together with others who reverenced Jesus as Lord. It was the result of the Holy Spirit's work of calling and gathering in her life.

Calling is a prelude to gathering. We used the example of a person receiving a telephone call about an illness in the family. The desired result of that call would be a gathering together of the family members. Similarly, the Holy Spirit has something in mind for those called by him. His further purpose is to join together those who have been called by the Gospel.

TOGETHER, HE CAN MAKE IT HAPPEN

"Together, we can make it happen." Do you remember that slogan? It was used nationwide in a secular appeal for funds. It is an optimistic boast that was used quite effectively, but it is not always true. Humanity can more honestly sing,

"Together, we *can't* make it happen." There are endless examples of the powerlessness of good intentions. If the little phrase really worked, would there still be wars, or only a shaky peace? Would race and color still cause separation? Would two-thirds of the world remain cold and hungry while others sleep badly under electric blankets, tossing with the discomforts of indigestion from too much food or drink? It seems that family quarreling, neighborhood bickering, town clashes, national rivalry and world unrest compose the truer version: "Together, we *can't* make it happen."

Christians have a different song: "Together, *He* can make it happen." Here are no false claims regarding our innate abilities. Unlike the little train in the children's story that huffs up the hill saying "I think I can, I think I can," the people of God make a strange and often misunderstood confession: "I know I can't, I know I can't." "I believe that I cannot by my own understanding or effort believe in Jesus Christ my Lord, or come to him, *but*," and then comes the good part. God has not left us in our helplessness. His Spirit accomplishes within us what we could not manufacture on our own, namely, a response of faith and a treasuring of togetherness.

In a small group one Sunday evening we were to respond individually to the question, "In what area of your life do you feel most defeated?" I had to admit that I was feeling most defeated in the use of my time. As a husband/father/pastor, I often found myself in a no-win situation. When I was at home, I felt convicted that I should be doing work at my desk, attending a meeting, making calls at the hospital, or visiting members in their homes. Then when I did these things, I felt guilty about not spending more time at home! Others shared their answers. Two people said that they felt defeat in every area of their lives. They had said it in the right place. It was exciting to see how the group loved them for their honesty and formed a caring support system around them. Here was no boast about how "We can make it happen." Those two had just admitted "We can't." But together, the group moved to the solid confidence that *He* can.

God never requires a single thing from us but what he stands ready to equip us to accomplish it. We are always and in all ways saved by grace. That is true of our salvation; it is also true when we need to control our temper while disciplining the children. It is true of forgiveness, and just as true when patience is needed toward someone interrupting our plans or schedule. Grace means that I lean on God for everything. He can make it happen, and it happens best together. The Holy Spirit calls, individually and personally. The Holy Spirit gathers, collectively and corporately.

Can you think of any hermit Christians in the New Testament? John the Baptist might come to mind, but he had a unique role in ushering in the Christian era. It is a futile search to scan the pages of Scripture to find someone shouting "I am a Christian and I want to be left all alone!" That's simply not the vocabulary of the early church. Rather, the big word is "together." The Book of Acts, especially chapters two and four, offers convincing evidence.

Even prior to the day of Pentecost, the Holy Spirit had done his work of gathering those early disciples in preparation for the power surge they would experience. "When the day of Pentecost had come, they were all *together* in one place" (Acts 2:1). If togetherness is intrinsic to spiritual power, there is much in our lifestyle that increases the odds against it. Families rarely spend significant time together. Even eating one meal all together as a family takes real determination and cooperation. Families of faith are also characterized more by apartness than by togetherness. Small bits and pieces assemble for study or service. One survey concluded that the most vital activity for congregational togetherness is the annual church bazaar! Even worship divides instead of unites. Two worship services in a congregation result in the equivalent of having two congregations. Seldom do building committees plan for facilities to house all members at one time and in one place. It is more practical to "plan to have more than one service if necessary." I wonder if Pentecost would have happened if the disciples had decided to meet in groups of 10 and in 12 different locations instead of all being together in the same house.

INTENTIONAL GATHERING

Soon the number of believers jumped from 120 to over three thousand, but the principle of togetherness prevailed. "And they *devoted* themselves to the apostles' teaching and fellowship, to the breaking of bread and the prayers" (Acts 2:42). Intentional gathering rated as highly as correct teaching. In any waves of revival or renewal throughout the church, there is an increase of intentional gathering. Deeper hunger for God's Word and greater involvement in prayer are accompanied by a more intense acknowledgment of the importance of Christian fellowship. The most growing and active congregations that I have observed include and emphasize opportunities for regular intentional gathering, usually including the sharing of a meal. Such emphasis is not original, but it is surely scriptural. "And all who believed were *together* and had all things in common; and they sold their possessions and goods and distributed them to all, as any had need. And day by day, attending the temple *together* and breaking bread in their homes, they partook of food with glad and generous hearts, praising God and having favor with all the people. And the Lord added to their number day by day those who were being saved" (Acts 2:44-47).

Acts, chapter four, continues the story of togetherness in the early church. It also includes the example of Peter and John as they were imprisoned for their preaching and then released with the warning to keep silent about Jesus. "When they were released they went to their friends" (Acts 4:23). Even the spiritual leaders were not above the need for personal sharing and support. Ordination is not a vaccine to immunize against the need for intimate Christian fellowship.

The Apostle Paul didn't fare very well on his lone journey to Damascus. At that time he was one mad man against the followers of the Way. After his conversion, he was infected with a desire for togetherness. His writings express this desire in words like "I am praying for you," "I am longing to see you," "I always remember you," "I am hoping that you can come and visit me or that I can come and visit you." Perhaps his greatest testimony to the treasure of togetherness is the last chapter of Romans. Here the most doctrinally and theologically solid letter that Paul ever wrote ends with a rather academically embarrassing list of plain greetings... a whole chapter of them! One would think that some early scholar would have considered these mundane hellos as unnecessary and deleted them long ago. But the Holy Spirit has both inspired and preserved the Word for us, and it includes this touching list of references to people who had had meaning in Paul's life. Christian gatherings have a glisten that not everyone detects.

An ongoing reminder is preserved in the words of Hebrews 10:24-25. "Let us consider how to stir up one another to love and good works, *not neglecting to meet together*, as is the habit of some, but encouraging one another, and all the more as you see the Day drawing near."

One of the most poignant laments of Jesus rises out of his desire to draw all his people together. "O Jerusalem, Jerusalem, killing the prophets and stoning those who are sent to you! How often would I have gathered your children together as a hen gathers her brood under her wings, and you would not!" (Matthew 23:37). When the Holy Spirit pursues his task of gathering, he shares a deep interest that resides in the heart of Jesus.

TOGETHER IN FELLOWSHIP

Together, he can make it happen. Just what does happen? For one thing, he makes a *fellowship* (koinonia) happen. It is like no other fellowship you have experienced. In most clubs or groups, you have to present credentials of success. In the Christian Church, you have to present credentials of failure. You have to be pretty good to get into some organizations. You have to be pretty bad to get into the church. In no other fellowship is there a regular opening exercise where sins, shortcomings and failures are confessed - and the spiritual leader initiates and joins in the confession! In many other associations, you have to wear a mask; you don't dare to be yourself and must not share either your heavy burdens or your joys. In this unique fellowship, however, there is the proper mix that allows you to be wrong, to be accepted, and to be encouraged toward what is right, all at the same time.

TOGETHER IN SERVICE

The Holy Spirit also makes *service* (diakonia) happen. This is a service like you never thought you could perform. The world offers distinguished service awards, but the Holy Spirit offers many undistinguished service opportunities. You end up doing ordinary things for extraordinary reasons. Doing them "as unto the Lord" makes for special service. He may call you to enormously challenging tasks and surprise you by fitting you for the job. However, when Jesus spoke of judgment in Matthew 25, he cited little things as evidence. A cup of cold water... a visit to a jail... remembering the sick... sharing needed clothing... such simple service pulses with the very heartbeat of God. One lady bakes an apple pie and brings it to a new family in her neighborhood. It is her way of letting Christ's love show through her. She will never be elected to any Council of Churches, but in the counsel of God, her humble service does not go unnoticed.

TOGETHER IN PROCLAMATION

Proclamation (kerygma) is a third happening of the Holy Spirit as he utilizes the gathered people of God. The gathered ones use the Creed to remind themselves of what they have to say to the world when they scatter. It is a unique message that tells of a Messiah born in a barn; a Prince, wandering and homeless; a Conqueror riding a donkey; a King crowned with thorns; a Lord nailed to a cross; a Savior in a borrowed tomb; a living but unseen God. Yet God's people continue this proclamation, and lives are changed by it.

The Holy Spirit is still gathering his church. Together, he makes all kinds of good things happen. An availability to the Holy Spirit will result in nothing less than the invasion of the kingdom of God into the hearts of people and, through them, into the world.

* * *

Note the "Think/Talk/Pray about section relating to Chapter 5.

CHAPTER SIX

The Holy Spirit in the Life of the Church...He Enlightens with His Gifts

What if your name was on the gift list of some King or Queen? Wouldn't you wonder about what you might receive? You have even more cause for wonder, anticipation, exhilaration. You are on God's gift list!

GIFT LISTS

God is by nature a giver, and his people are gifted people. There are a number of "gift lists" in the Bible. The Ten Commandments are a gift list. Every commandment is a guard which the Lord has placed around a gift he has given. The gifts include himself, his name, communication with him in worship, parents, life, family, possessions, reputation and neighbors. Instead of thinking of the commandments as cold, legal rules, they may be looked upon as gracious clues regarding the protection of beautiful gifts God has given us.

Individual people compose another inventory of gifts God has given. Once, while talking about gifts, I walked around in the audience and put ribbons and bows on people. It was an exercise in gift wrapping. Everyone was encouraged to look upon each other as a gift. The people were reminded to look down at the ribbons that wound around them so that they would see themselves as gifts too.

There are things we refer to as "natural endowments" that are more properly credited as being gifts from God. Talents

50

for singing, sewing, speaking, welding, listening, cooking, building, farming, repairing are all part of a gift list. It pays the Giver no compliment to modestly deny having them or to not recognize them. Rather, they call for grateful awareness, joyful celebration, and responsible employment of the gifts for the blessing of self and others.

Still another gift list deals with "positional" gifts in the Church, such as the "apostles, prophets, evangelists, pastors, teachers" mentioned in Ephesians 4:12.

Although all these gift lists are worth much more consideration, we will concern ourselves with yet another list. This one contains what is usually referred to as "spiritual gifts." Even here we will be arbitrary, for several of these lists are found in Scripture. One is in the book of Romans, chapter 12. A hymn to the Holy Spirit refers to this list:

"Plenteous of grace, descend from high
Rich in thy sevenfold energy.. (SBH #124)
This is poetic reference to the gifts of prophesy, service, teaching, exhortation, contributions, aid and mercy.

Other hymns speak of gifts, but without specific number:

"Come, Holy Spirit, God and Lord;
Be all thy gifts in plenty poured
To save, to strengthen and make whole
Each ready mind, each waiting soul." (SBH #122)

"Come, Holy Ghost, in love,
Shed on us from above
Thine own bright ray;
Divinely good thou art;
Thy sacred gifts impart
To gladden each sad heart;
O come today." (SBH #121)

"That word above all earthly powers,
No thanks to them, abideth;
The Spirit and the gifts are ours
Through him who with us sideth.." (SBH #150)

WHAT ARE THESE GIFTS?

The list we shall follow is found in 1st Corinthians, chapter 12. There are two reasons for choosing this list. First, it mentions the greatest number (nine of them). Second, it is the most controversial list when spiritual gifts are considered.

All the gifts in this list can be seen as specific and particular aids. They do not deal with general, all-embracing needs. For example, when the spiritual gift of knowledge is given, it is not a kind of "knowing-all-there-is-to-know" about God. Likewise, the gift of faith does not here mean that kind of faith which is unto salvation. All these gifts relate to smaller matters than the "full counsel of God."

Let's note the gifts which the Apostle Paul lists in 1st Corinthians 12:8-10.

"To one is given through the Spirit the utterance of *wisdom*, and to another the utterance of *knowledge* according to the same Spirit, to another *faith* by the same Spirit, to another gifts of *healing* by the one Spirit, to another the working of *miracles*, to another *prophecy*, to another the *ability to distinguish between spirits*, to another various kinds of *tongues*, to another the *interpretation of tongues*."

Because the Holy Spirit uses these gifts for the enlightenment and blessing of the Church, they may be thought of as nine "turn ons" given to help edify the people of God. As we consider a definition of each gift, I will also give an example of it operating in the life and ministry of Jesus. You can decide whether the examples are sound and helpful, or whether I am stretching Scripture to do this. I am not able to give examples from the life of Jesus in the case of tongues or their interpretation. I suppose one could flee to Jesus' divinity and say there were no tongues unknown to him. I would rather, however, seek examples coming from Jesus as a true man relying upon what was made available to him by his Father through the Spirit. As such, he scores seven out of nine - not bad!

TURN ON #1 - *Wisdom* is knowledge well-applied to a situation for the sake of counseling or instruction. Jesus exhibited this gift in answering a question of his disciples about who is the greatest in the kingdom of heaven (Matt. 18:1-4) and in confounding his critics (Matt. 21:23-27).

TURN ON #2 - *Knowledge* is information about a matter that is given without special investigation or study. When Jesus directed the catching of a fish with a coin in its mouth (Matt. 17:27), he was not employing a kind of X-ray vision that penetrated soil, sand, water, and bone structure. He simply spoke with a knowledge that it would be there, and it was.

TURN ON #3 - This kind of *faith* is the daring to ask or to do. It is the kind that doesn't flinch at moving mountains (Matt. 17:20) or even facing the dangers of suffering and martyrdom (Mark 8:31-33). Peter is a classic example of human hesitation in boldly exercising this gift, even with the Lord's encouragement (Matt. 14:28-33).

TURN ON #4 - The gift of *healing* is faith directed toward the alleviation of physical diseases and disabilities. There is no shortage of instances of healing done by Jesus (Luke 7:21).

TURN ON #5 - *Miracles* involve faith directed to seeking God's intervention in specific situations other than healing. Cursing the fig tree (Matt. 21:18-22) and multiplying the loaves and fish (Matt. 15:32-39) are samples of the many nature miracles Jesus performed.

TURN ON #6 - *Prophecy*, as a spiritual gift, does not have the broad dimension of prophecy defined as foretelling or forthtelling. It is rather the announcement of a more specific, pertinent revelation or message received from the Lord. It will not contradict Scripture, and its worth is usually properly authenticated by its hearers. Jesus made a prophetic announcement in the synagogue when he read from Isaiah and then told the hearers that those words had been fulfilled in him that very day (Luke 4:21). As seen in this example, a single prophecy can stir a varied response from the audience (Luke 4:22,29).

TURN ON #7 - The *ability to distinguish between spirits* deals with having a sensitivity regarding whether the origin of something is good or evil, from God or the Devil. While others might be fooled by outer appearances, Jesus knew the hearts of people (Mark 2:5-8).

TURN ON #8 - Various kinds of *tongues* consist of an

unlearned voicing of sounds which, though unintelligible, are used in a personal and private prayer or praise experience with God. Their only proper use in public would be when made intelligible by interpretation.

TURN ON #9 - *Interpretation of tongues* occurs when the meaning of uttered tongues is made helpful to others by the message being restated in the language understood by the group.

WHAT THE GIFTS ARE *NOT* FOR

These gifts are not for salvation. They must not be taken as evidence for whether a person is saved or not saved. They are distinctly meant for believers, but they are not meant to distinguish "real" Christians from those who only pose as Christians. A terrible and ugly misuse is made of the gifts if their presence or absence is made a basis for judgments such as "You certainly are no Christian if you have not experienced the gifts," or on the other hand, "I don't believe any Christian would mess around with those weird things they call spiritual gifts." The gifts are not badges to wear as indications that you are an authentic member of the household of God (or of the household of Satan, depending upon your point of view).

The gifts also are not for providing status symbols to be used within the fellowship of the Church. They are not little playing pieces in a game to show who are the favorites of the heavenly Father. Just a little twist is all that is necessary to make something good into something bad. This happens when a spiritual gift is twisted into something that puffs up the individual instead of building up the Body of Christ. In spiritual circles, the old taunt "My pa's better than your papa" becomes "My pa's better to me than he is to you!" This implies that the heavenly Father knows best and that he gives the best grades to the best of his children. The spiritual gifts are thus twisted into becoming part of the grading system.

WHAT THE GIFTS *ARE* FOR

The gifts are for service, not for status. It is no accident that Paul, right after listing the gifts, launches into a teaching that uses the human body as an example (1st Cor. 12:12-26). There is no single part of the body that exists by and for itself. Any part that quits functioning helpfully toward other parts is likely diseased or paralyzed. Likewise, no spiritual gift is solely for self-edification. Speaking in tongues comes the closest to being this, as we shall discuss later. All the rest are obviously meant for the good of others. No one is to exercise wisdom or knowledge in a vacuum. Faith is not for individual escapade. Healing and other miracles presuppose others being helped by them. So do prophecy, discernment and interpretation. The gifts are for service.

The gifts are tools. Suppose I plan to have a garden. The soil has to be prepared for planting. I could use my bare hands to break up the ground, but I would rather use tools that are available to me. I use shovel, fork, and rake. I continue to use tools to drive stakes for straight rows and to make holes or trenches for seed. The tools are utilized for weeding, thinning, and, finally, for harvesting. While my garden is growing nicely, and especially when the fruit and vegetables are about ready for eating, people may express interest in my garden. I encourage them to come over. When they respond, I don't take them into the tool shed and show them shovels and rakes. Though the tools have been helpful, they are not for display. It is the fruit on the plant that more properly gets the attention. If there was nothing growing in my garden, it would be a bit strange to take the visitors to the shed and say, "Well, after all, the tools are the important thing. Whether the garden produces is of little significance." On the other hand, neither should the visitors degrade my tools or scold me for using them. Spiritual gifts are tools. As such, they have special purpose but they are not ends in themselves. They are means to good ends and purposes.

They can also be looked upon as vehicles. Suppose that Glacier National Park is 175 miles west of where I live. I can go down to the depot, get on the train and ride to the park. Glacier is my destination. One does not get on a train just to be and to stay on the train. It is a vehicle by which to get somewhere. While I am riding on the train, I look out the window and see a car and a plane heading west. Should I shake my head and think that I am the only one who will reach the park? Of course not! The car and plane are also authentic vehicles for getting there. The train, which is my present form of transportation, is not the only way. However, it would also be foolish for someone to stand on the depot platform and ridicule people traveling by train, especially if the platform critic had never been on a train. So it is with spiritual gifts. They are only vehicles used with destinations in mind, but they are authentic vehicles and should be acknowledged as such.

A problem remains for much of the church, however. We have a garden to plant. Tools are accessible, but some don't know what they are, others fail to use them properly, and still others refuse to even consider using them. We have a goal and destination, but the available vehicles are often ignored or argued about instead of being used for really getting someplace. St. Paul cites both problem and solution in 1st Corinthians 2:12- 14. "Now we have received not the spirit of the world, but the Spirit which is from God, that we might understand the gifts bestowed on us by God. And we impart this in words not taught by human wisdom but taught by the Spirit, interpreting spiritual truths to those who possess the Spirit. The unspiritual man does not receive the gifts of the Spirit of God, for they are folly to him, and he is not able to understand them because they are spiritually discerned." God is on our side and at our side to make his gifts the effective treasure he intended them to be among his people.

HOW ARE THEY RECEIVED?

The spiritual gifts are not earned. They are offered freely and bestowed graciously at the Spirit's discretion. We must not stifle the Holy Spirit's gracious action by refusing the gifts, being uninterested in them, or closing our minds to them. Nor must we seek to coerce him into giving us a particular gift in a prescribed manner at a specified time and for a guaranteed period. The proper stance is to be receptive, available, open, interested, eager, grateful as you would be regarding any wonderful gift that is potentially yours.

Trust is how you receive the spiritual gifts. You trust Jesus for being saved, forgiven. Likewise, you trust the Holy Spirit for equipping you to serve and for bestowing upon you whatever will bless the fellowship. You don't think up some wise words to say - you trust the Holy Spirit to give you wisdom. You don't make plans to engineer some kind of miracle - you trust the Holy Spirit to perform it. You don't go around making judgments that sentence people to heaven or hell - you trust the Holy Spirit to sensitize you to knowing whether something is of God's leading or Satan's tempting. You don't manufacture a bunch of babbling sounds, or make up your own translation of a message - you trust the Holy Spirit to give you sounds of prayer and praise, or the meaning expressed by such sounds. Grace and trust mark every facet of your life with God, whether your initial coming into his kingdom, or your growth and service as a member of it.

WHY IS THERE NOT A GREATER NUMBER EXPERIENCING THE GIFTS?

One reason for not experiencing the spiritual gifts is that we may not be aware that they are available to us. A good program may be on the radio. A special drama may be on television. A fine concert may take place in a local auditorium. They are all available to us, but we may miss every one of them simply by not being aware of them. The first task of evangelism is to make people aware of the Gospel. They still may not repent and believe, but they certainly will not if they never know what is available to them in Jesus. Likewise, a broad unawareness of the spiritual gifts will limit the experiencing of them throughout the Church.

There may, however, be an awareness of them without an accompanying desire for them. We may be well aware of a next-door neighbor, but never desire to have him inside our home. He may be somewhat strange. He may not have background or tastes similar to ours. He may have family or relatives who make us apprehensive, and once we invite him in, who knows but what it may be difficult to control when he comes again and the ones he may bring along with him!

The spiritual gifts can be threatening neighbors. Certain ones may be all right, but others make us uncomfortable. We don't like the company that some of them keep. Some of the gifts seem uncontrollable. Others are not part of our past experience and seem strange to us. Still others have been part of troublesome scenes we wish to avoid. A lack of desire, for reasons both bad and understandable, can make the gifts more scarce.

Besides the problems of awareness and desire, there is the matter of insensitivity. The gifts are around us more than we realize. We are insensitive to them because we have bought into mind-sets that rule out the activity of the Spirit in our midst. For example, a little lady attends a Bible study. She sits all evening with a question she doesn't ask, or with a comment she never makes. She feels the question is stupid and the comment isn't worth anyone's attention. She never considers that the Lord may be giving her a word of knowledge in that comment, or a word of wisdom in that question which might cause the entire group to focus upon something significant for all of them. Someone else in the group has an urge to say something, but stifles it. The group has never considered the possibility of a word of prophecy being spoken at their meeting, so they don't know that they may have missed a special message.

Church councils meet and are guided by Robert's Rules of Order. Proper motions are made, discussed, and voted upon. The minutes read like any other secular business meeting, noting every item as moved, seconded, and carried. The minutes never read: "Mr. Smith felt that the Lord was prompting him to lay the matter of increased missions giving before the council. The council accepted this as a possible leading from the Lord. Prayer and sharing took place in order to reach a consensus. When the matter was settled, there was full agreement that the Lord's will would more properly be done if the missions goal were doubled."

A worship service is in progress. Nothing is allowed to happen that is not in the bulletin. Spontaneous words or prayers from worshippers are considered inappropriate.

Silence is embarrassing and means only one thing - someone is missing a cue! A revelation, tongue, interpretation, silence, and prophecy are all mentioned by St. Paul in his description of Christian worship (1 Cor. 14:26). I wonder when all this stopped and bulletins began?! At one service I was conducting, a lady overcame her inhibitions during the offering, came up to the microphone and spoke a prophetic word. I didn't know quite how to handle it, since it was not a typical occurrence at a Lutheran service - so I printed it in the next Sunday's bulletin!

Another arena where we may be unaware of God's activity is in our minds. The mind is one of God's most precious gifts, but we fit our minds into a psychological framework instead of a biblical one. Then we wonder "Why doesn't God speak to us like he did to people in the Bible?" Instead of entertaining the possibility of God engaging our brains for giving us special, spontaneous, spiritual insight, we speak of "thoughts that just came to mind" or "ideas that struck us." In fact, if anyone uses a biblical orientation and mentions something that "the Lord said" to him, we wonder just who he thinks he is, or we worry that he is going off some religious deep end! I personally don't know how to manufacture an idea. When a helpful one comes to me, the best I can do is thank the Lord for it and put it to some good use. Of all the spiritual gifts, tongues is the only one that seems to bypass the mind. All the rest of the gifts involve the mind in their perception and implementation.

Lack of awareness and desire keep the gifts from being appropriated. Lack of sensitivity keeps them from being perceived. How sad that the biggest Giver of all, the Holy Spirit, remains such a stranger in his Church. How sad that his good gifts have been ignored, or even labeled as weird, odd, wild, bizarre.

TONGUES - THE TROUBLEMAKER

The most troublesome gift seems to be tongues. Tongues was experienced by all the Apostles (Acts 2), and Paul spoke in tongues more than anyone else in his day (1 Cor. 14:18).

Despite this, there is a tendency to run a pencil through the mention of this gift and rule it out. It is one of the lesser gifts, but not for the reason often given. Those who refer to it as such say that it is negligible because it appears toward the end of Paul's list. This is not a reliable argument. If you ask me to name my children, I may say "Paul, John, and Philip." Don't accuse me of loving Philip least because I named him last. I simply started with the oldest and went to the youngest. Next time, I may start with Phil, but that will not prove that I have now changed to loving Paul the least. Leveling similar judgment against St. Paul is equally unfair and unwise. In fact, Paul gives another list in 1st Corinthians 13:13 and what he mentions last is not least but greatest. "So faith, hope, and love abide, these three; but the greatest of these is love."

I would still agree, however, that tongues is one of the lesser gifts because it is used mostly for personal benefit and blessing. The rest of the gifts are predominantly for the blessing of others instead of only the one exercising the gift. Nevertheless, the gift of tongues should be valued, not despised. Through this gift, it is as though God says, "Let's start in the shallows. For more assurance of my close presence with you, I will give you special sounds to use in personal moments of prayer and praise to me. Perhaps this will encourage you and cause you to take my hand more firmly and let me lead you out of the shallows and into greater depths of discipleship and service."

It is like a child learning from a father. Dad spends hours teaching his little baby to make a sound. Finally the child says something that resembles "Daddy." The father is in ecstasy! He wants the child to say it over and over again. The proud father spreads the word that his young child has learned to talk. Well, not really. Some ungracious person could listen to the baby and ridicule the pronunciation. The baby could be criticized for using a word without even knowing a thing about the concept of fatherhood. The whole event could be crossed out as being nonsense and without meaning, but the father wouldn't agree. It has been a most exciting event of relationship. Soon the sounds expand, and the child is saying "Daddy, I love you." The child has no more a concept of "love" than he had of "father." He is simply giving back again the sounds the father gave him. There is no rational significance, yet there is great relational import here.

But now suppose several fathers are training their babies to talk. Then they get an idea. They will have a contest. Each father will bring his baby out on a stage and have the child say "Daddy, I love you." The crowd will vote on which baby should receive the prize for saying it the best! Wouldn't that be ridiculous? The sounds were not meant for winning contests. That would be a violation of their intent. It would spoil a good experience. The gift of tongues is not meant for contest purposes either, but there is a valid way that it enhances the relationship between Father and child, and it is neither necessary nor wise to censure it.

THE GIFTS AND THE GIVER

Finally, some words must be added about the gifts and the Giver. First, *the gifts are meant to bless the Church.* They are not intended to be a matter of competition among the members. They are given to complete and complement the whole Body of Christ.

Secondly, *we are to love the Giver, not be infatuated with the gifts.* When I asked Pauline to marry me, I offered her a diamond ring. I wanted her to say "Yes" because she loved me, not because she was infatuated with the ring. The Holy Spirit has the same desire as he offers gifts to his Church.

Thirdly, *the gifts come because we have the Giver; the Giver does not come through the gifts.* The Holy Spirit is the medium for the gifts; the gifts are not the medium for the Spirit. As part of an anniversary celebration, you may receive a gift because a *person* has first given himself/herself to you. Likewise, the Holy Spirit has first given himself to us; then he enlightens us with his gifts. We use the gifts as a celebration of the Giver.

* * *

Note the "Think/Talk/Pray about" section relating to Chapter 6.

CHAPTER SEVEN

The Holy Spirit in the Life of the Church...He Sanctifies

The first time I tried skiing, I went up on the lift and had to get down the mountain by myself. It was a terrifying experience. The next time, I went with an instructor whose presence and coaching gave me security and encouragement. What an improvement over going it alone!

Christians may have mountaintop experiences, but then are tricked into thinking that they must now go it alone as a way of proving their worth. This can lead to a terrifying schuss into a valley of despair. The truth is that an Instructor is available, and his presence and help make all the difference. After a brief summary, we will explore the difference the Holy Spirit makes in a Christian's everyday life.

A HOLY SPIRIT SHORT COURSE

A short course on the Holy Spirit could consist of five points:

Point #1 - You can't go wrong emphasizing the Holy Spirit. It is his day in the Church. It has been so since the day of Pentecost. Jesus was not being modest when he said, "It is to your advantage that I go away." He was being realistic and wise. "For if I do not go away, the Counselor will not come to you; but if I go, I will send him to you" (John 16:7). God has continually improved upon his presence with his people. The Father sent his Son to be a real presence, though temporary and local. The Son's departure ushered in the Holy Spirit's coming as an always and everywhere presence. The day of the Holy Spirit in the Church continues until Christ's return, when we shall see God clearly in undiminished glory.

Point #2 - You can't go wrong emphasizing the Spirit's work of making Jesus real in the hearts of believers. There need not be a concern that the Holy Spirit will steal the show from Jesus. The Spirit himself understands his own work too well to let that happen. "Jesus is Lord" on the lips and in the heart of a believer is the greatest compliment that can be paid to the Holy Spirit. That confession gives evidence that the Holy Spirit has done his work well.

Point #3 - You can't go wrong emphasizing our need of the Holy Spirit's power for service and witness. There is no other power supply, and to despise this solitary source is to commit spiritual suicide. To blaspheme the Spirit is like an electric motor pulling its own plug out of the socket. Jesus' admonition still holds: "You shall receive power when the Holy Spirit has come upon you" (Acts 1:8).

Point #4 - You *can* go wrong with undue emphasis upon the gifts. The Church needs to grow more in the awareness of these gifts and become experientially comfortable with them. It must always be kept in mind, however, that they are enablers and not ends in themselves.

Point #5 - You can't go wrong emphasizing the fruit of the Holy Spirit. The greatest fruit is love. As a mark of his sanctifying activity, the Holy Spirit leaves a trail of loving disciples.

"SONKIST" DISCIPLES

Sanctification may be pictured as an arrow ascending at an upward angle(↗). It is like a cloning process of becoming more like Christ Jesus. Jesus cannot be reduced to a list of attributes, but when St. Paul itemizes the fruit of the Spirit in Galatians 5:22-23, he is really describing Jesus. No one else has so completely exhibited "love, joy, peace, patience, kindness, goodness, faithfulness, gentleness, self-control." The fruit of the Spirit results in the believer resembling Jesus, taking on the characteristics of Jesus by having the Christ recreated within.

When Jesus said, "By this my Father is glorified, that you bear much fruit, and so prove to be my disciples" (John 15:8), he was not encouraging entries for some kind of fruit fair involving judging and awarding of appropriate ribbons. Rather, the Father's heart is made glad when there is evidence that his family is maturing, and the best sign of this is the growing family resemblance to the elder brother Jesus.

I like to describe sanctified saints as "Sonkist disciples." Our lives are meant to show that they have been intimately touched by Jesus, affected and changed by him. The orange industry has seen fit to brand their product; I would suggest a brand for all Christians to wear. Unfortunately, the word "charismatic" has gone the route of many a good word and has become a negative term used in branding people. So I would like to spell the word "χarismatic", and use it as a positive mark upon all Christians. Using the ancient Greek "Chi" for Christ in that Spirit-connected word becomes a constant reminder of the basic and ultimate goal of the Spirit as he demonstrates his power and presence in the Church. The Holy Spirit is no small businessman who goes around injecting occasional gifts into the experience of believers. He is in the big business of transforming the whole Body into the likeness of Christ. "Sunkist" on an orange should be more than a label or surface coloring. It is supposed to assure inner flavor and juiciness. "Sonkist" also means more than surface tinkering. It deals with deep, inner reconstruction out of which emanates evidence that our natural ways have been improved upon by the Spirit. This evidence or proof of discipleship shows what company we have been keeping. It bears witness that we have been with Jesus, have learned from him, have been indwelt by him, and are exhibiting traits that resemble him.

THE TOP THREE FRUITS

What St. Paul put at the end of the list in 1st Corinthians 13, he puts at the top of the list in Galatians. Love heads the list, then joy and peace join love to make a kind of "top three."

"As the Father has loved me, so have I loved you; abide in my love" (John 15:9). Jesus makes love sound like an ocean. He says "Swim in my ocean of love. Splash in it. Wash in it. Be buoyed up by it." He makes it sound like an air mass. "Let it surround you. Inhale it. Exhale it. It is indispensable to your being." He makes it sound like a place to live. "Operate within its framework. Let it be a place to come into and come back to. It is a stable foundation under all that you are and do." The greatest fruit of the Spirit is love. It is to permeate every action in the believer's life. One of the best definitions I know is this: "Love is the determination to bless, with all that you have and with all that you are" (Source unknown).

Second of the top three is joy. "These things I have spoken to you, that my joy may be in you, and that your joy may be full" (John 15:11). We can plan a celebration. We can announce when it shall begin and estimate when it shall end. All celebrations come to an end.. all but one. The celebration begun by the joy of Jesus keeps going and going. Most celebrations are "because of" parties. The celebration which Jesus causes in the heart is an "in spite of" party. It continues whether things go right or wrong. The celebration also occurs in the strangest places. A poem shows a celebration going on in the midst of the tiring and tiresome work of a cotton field:

"There's a king and a captain high,
And he's coming by and by,
And he'll find me hoeing cotton when he comes.
You can hear his legions charging
In the regions of the sky,
And he'll find me hoeing cotton when he comes.

There's a man they thrust aside,
Who was tortured till he died,
And he'll find me hoeing cotton when he comes.
He was hated and rejected,
He was scorned and crucified,
And he'll find me hoeing cotton when he comes.

When he comes! When he comes!
He'll be crowned by saints and angels when he comes.
They'll be shouting out Hosanna!
To the man that men denied,
And I'll kneel among my cotton when he comes."
(Author unknown - From "The Daily Study Bible" by
William Barclay, Gospel of Matthew, Vol.2, page 351)

Do you catch the sense of deep, quiet celebration going on in that cotton field? The joy of Jesus ignites and fuels such celebration. Sonkist disciples are standing invitations for others to join the party.

The third fruit is peace. "Peace I leave with you; my peace I give to you. Let not your hearts be troubled, neither let them be afraid" (John 14:27). I remember seeing a picture entitled "Peace." A rocky coastline is being battered by hard, crashing waves. In the center of this turbulence sits a tiny, unruffled bird in the crevice of a rock. That's it, isn't it? You recognize it as the kind of peace that only God can give. St. Paul describes it as a peace that passes understanding, yet a peace not past experiencing, for it keeps our hearts and minds in Christ Jesus (Phil. 4:7).

Love.. joy.. peace. They form a trinity coming from the Trinity. The love of the Father, the joy of the Son, and the peace of the Spirit invade the lives of those they touch. These primary three seem to actuate all the rest of the fruits as spin offs: "patience, kindness, goodness, faithfulness, gentleness, self-control." Like the nine gifts of the Spirit, the nine fruits of the Spirit evolve into selfless blessing to others.

TRUSTING VERSUS TRYING

It is easy to make the mistake of letting the fruits be a list of things to work for or to work at. It is clear that justification, being made right with God, is by grace through faith. Justification is a "done-for-you" project. But then it is quite possible to let sanctification, growth in Christlikeness, become a "do-it-yourself" project. Having been saved by grace alone, we set out to prove to God by our actions that we were, after all, well worth the saving!

Jesus said, "I am the vine, you are the branches. He who abides in me, and I in him, he it is that bears much fruit, *for apart from me you can do nothing*" (John 15:5). Do you believe Jesus when he says "nothing"? That means you cannot *save* yourself. It also means you cannot *shape* yourself. Many nonchurchgoers with problems have intentions of someday shaping up and coming to church. My answer is that if they can shape up by themselves, they do not need to come to church. Their intentions to shape up indicate that they are convinced they can do it themselves apart from any help or strength of the Lord.

It is not, however, only nonchurched people who think this way. Many churchgoing Christians put sanctification into a category of "trying to" - trying to be more loving, trying to be more joyful, trying to have more peace of mind, trying to be more patient. But *it is the Holy Spirit who sanctifies.* The Scriptures mention the need to be filled with the Holy Spirit, not with good intentions. Imagine visiting an orchard where the air is filled with sounds of grunting and groaning. You ask the orchard keeper about the noise. He tells you that it is coming from all the fruit trees that are trying hard to make the fruit pop out of their branches! When sanctification is thought to be a process of "trying to," the Church becomes an equally ridiculous orchard.

Sanctification is a matter of "trusting for," not "trying to." Yes, we are back to the business of trust again. Sanctification is not performance, but appropriation. For the Devil to be successful, he need only keep you from depending and drawing upon the power of the Holy Spirit. You will then attempt things in your own strength, and you will be no match for Satan. He is in trouble, however, if you meet him by relying on the Holy Spirit who supplies a matching and surpassing power to resist the Devil.

Let me contrast the difference between trying and trusting. Take patience as an example. Suppose one of my boys gets into some trouble. I realize that we will have to talk about it, but this time I determine to be a patient and understanding father. I will hear the boy out before making any comment. So my boy begins. Soon it becomes obvious that he is padding some details to make the best possible case for himself. I begin to inwardly react to this attempted snow job. Since I have determined to be patient, however, I hold my tongue. Pretty soon the pressure builds up within me so that I am having trouble concentrating on what he is saying. The problem he is involved in could easily have been avoided had he only remembered what I have told him a thousand times before! Finally I can contain myself no longer and I explode. Patience will have to wait for another occasion. I intended to be patient, but it didn't work. Even if it had sort of worked, I would have been so concerned about trying to be patient that I would not have heard my son's explanation.

Trusting leads down a different path. I begin by having a short, silent conversation with the Lord. "Lord, you know and I know that this situation calls for something I simply don't have, namely, patience. Out of your abundance, you supply my every need. Patience is one of your fruits, not mine. I know that, through your Spirit, you can provide me with just the amount I need for this situation. Thanks, Lord." Such trusting releases me from the pressure of producing patience and frees me to give my attention to understanding what gave rise to the problem.

The fruit of the Spirit is not born out of a determination that stubbornly maintains "I will!" Rather, the finest prelude to the bearing of spiritual fruit is the confession "I can't!" The one exhibits a "trying" stance, while the other reveals a posture of trusting. One is performance-centered, the other is appropriation-centered. One pastor put it this way: "My life in the Spirit took on an exciting new dimension when I stopped saying 'please' and started saying 'thanks.'" Thanks expresses the greater trust beforehand that the Lord will provide. "Please" leaves you still in the problem and without a solution. "Thanks" shows that you have already trusted God to give you what is necessary to deal with a situation.

An old liturgical refrain says, "Cleanse the thoughts of our hearts by the inspiration of thy Holy Spirit." That inspiration includes embarking on new adventures of trust, leaving behind the old methods of carnal trying. When you have lustful, hateful or hurtful thoughts, don't depend upon yourself to cleanse your mind and get to thinking about something else. Use the words of that old prayer, or similar ones of your own, as a way of commending the problem to God the Holy Spirit. You can relax trustingly in having given over the responsibility to the One capable of dealing with it. He will bring new thoughts that will cast out the others in a way that you could never bring about by your own cleverness.

INSTANT FRUIT

If grunting and groaning fruit trees violate the picture of an orchard, so does the picture of trees with instant, ripe fruit popping out of their branches. The process of budding, blossoming, and developing fruit does not insult the Creator. It is his way of investing time in a good thing. Even when trusting replaces trying, sanctification is a process and not instantaneous. Improvement may be immediate, but improvement is not instant perfection. A subtle form of the same old game of trying is that of trying to trust for all the fruit of the Spirit in one glorious grab!

DEALING WITH DISAPPOINTMENT IN OTHERS

We may be bothered when we fail to see instant fruit in others. I remember seeing a picture of a skinny creature in a barebranched tree in Africa. Looking closer, I discovered that it was an emaciated woman picking new buds off this tree in a famine stricken area. Her frantic efforts were insuring the absence of any fruit in the future. It is possible to treat young or immature Christians in the same way. Instead of treating these budding ones in Christ with kindness and gentleness, they get picked off by criticism or by being given too much responsibility before their proper time.

One pastor admitted to his impatience with teenage Christians. Then he learned a lesson in a dream as the Lord conducted him on a tour of fields at various stages of development. Would he expect a harvest from a field newly sown, or from one where the heads were only forming? Then neither should he expect fully developed fruit in the lives of new or young Christians.

I like to return to the picture of the orchard. Can you imagine one tree swatting another because the fruit on this other tree's branches was slightly greener than on its own? Instead, let's imagine one more advanced tree speaking encouragingly to a younger tree, assuring it that in time there would also be good, ripe fruit on its branches. It is not difficult to sense which kind of orchard the Church should be.

An old Hawaiian man was planting peanuts. He gave each seed the same careful attention, patting the soft dirt with his bare feet in such a precise way that the ground looked like a patchwork quilt. His little piece of ground was divided into four sections. The peanuts were planted at different times of the year so that some were ready for harvest, some were quite well matured, others were new plants, and the fourth section was newly seeded. He knew the exact care each section required to insure continued growth. He was a reminder to me of how the Holy Spirit works within the varied garden of the Church (and of all the different nuts he has to work with?!).

DEALING WITH DISAPPOINTMENT IN OUR-SELVES

Moses is my favorite example of how to deal with disappointment. He keenly desired to enter the land God had promised him. But Moses struck out at Meribah (Numbers 20). The people were grumbling about having no water. The Lord told Moses to tell the rock to yield water for them. This would assure the people that the Lord cared for them. However, Moses' impatience with the people caused him to give his own twist to the scene. He apparently didn't believe what the Lord said about the rock, so he said something like this: "You rebels! What do you expect me to do, make water flow from this rock?" Then he struck the rock twice with his rod - and out gushed water! Moses' eyes were probably bigger than anyone's!

The Lord's discipline seems harsh. He told Moses and

Aaron that because they doubted him, their feet would not touch the promised land. What a disappointment that must have been. But neither Moses nor Aaron threw down their gloves and walked off the field. Aaron walked up Mount Hor, installed his son as priest, and died. Moses composed a song (in which lofty praise is given to the Lord his *Rock*), blessed each tribe, went up Mount Nebo, looked at the land he would never enter, died, and was eulogized like no other man (Deut. 34:10-12). There is a grand example in the way that disappointment did not end the relationship between God and Moses. Moses' failures kept him from going to Israel, but didn't prevent him from going to heaven. In fact, Moses finally did set foot in the promised land in a rather unusual way. He was with Jesus on the Mount of Transfiguration (Matt. 17:3).

Disappointments in life need not write "Disappointment" across all of life. Self-control does not only involve keeping us from doing wrong. It also involves keeping us from resenting others who disappoint us, and from becoming defensive or depressed when we are the failures. Being a Christian is knowing what it is like to fall and to be picked up again. Sanctification does not mean never stumbling. It means going on despite the stumbling. It means having a confidence that though we fail, the Holy Spirit is on hand to deal with power failure.

"If we live by the Spirit, let us also walk by the Spirit" (Gal. 5:25). You walk one step at a time. But you keep walking, and as you do, your life shows signs that you are a Sonkist disciple, that your life has been intimately touched by Jesus. That's the Holy Spirit, the Sanctifier, at work.

* * *

Note the "Think/Talk/Pray about" section relating to Chapter 7.

CHAPTER EIGHT

The Holy Spirit in the Life of the Church...He Keeps

LET GO! I'VE GOT YOU!

My middle son, John, was eager to learn how to swim. He was not eager to let go of the side of the pool. He became a three-quarter swimmer. He would kick with both feet, but use only one arm to paddle. The other hand carefully held onto the side of the pool. "Let go, John. Daddy's got you. Let go. I've got you!" Over and over I would give this assurance to a little boy who wanted to make very sure the water was not going to go over his head. But he was dealing with more than water. He was wrestling with the question of whether Dad was really up to the task of keeping him from sinking. Eventually, as he gained confidence in my care, he also lost his fear of deep water.

Some people, including some people in the church, are afraid of, or at least are somewhat skittish about, the Holy Spirit. The Comforter makes them uncomfortable. The Counselor disturbs them. They are skeptical about the Spirit of Truth. They think that they can get along without the Holy Spirit's presence and power even though Peter couldn't, Paul couldn't, and Jesus himself couldn't. I can identify with those same fears, apprehensions, and threatened feelings. Entrusting myself to the third person in the Trinity was more difficult than becoming at ease with the Father and Son. I was no small child at the time. I was a pastor, ordained for 15 years. Yet I was clinging to the edge of the pool with one hand, afraid both of deeper water and of the One who kept patiently saying to me "Let go, Rod. I've got you!" John, not without some trepidation, let go of the edge of the pool and is now glad that he did. I'm glad I did too. It was a necessary move that led to knowing the Holy Spirit's caring capability as keeper.

I also identify with the story of how monkeys are trapped. A small-necked container with a few peanuts inside it is firmly fastened to the ground. Eventually, a monkey comes along, sticks his hand into the container, and grabs the peanuts. However, he cannot get his hand back out as long as he holds the peanuts in his fist. Instead of losing the peanuts, he loses his freedom. By not letting go of the peanuts, he forsakes the wealth and wonder of the entire jungle.

It is possible to hold onto only a smattering of teaching picked up in Christian education as a child and not grasp greater opportunities for spiritual growth as an adult. It is possible to settle for a documented historical act, such as baptism or confirmation, without having any current, daily relational contact with the Lord. We may cling to a preferred life style we do not want changed. There may be certain attitudes or prejudices we don't care to have disturbed. Like the monkey, we sit trapped with a few peanuts in our hand and fail to experience a much fuller, richer, and more exciting life with God because we won't let go.

We must return to the solid ground of Luther's explanation to the Third Article of the Creed. "I believe that I cannot by my own reason or effort... *but the Holy Spirit.*" Buying into this explanation necessitates a letting go of our own personal strategies, and relying confidently upon the Spirit's strong promise of "I've got you." It is in anticipation of that satisfying assurance that God speaks as an encouraging Father: "Let go. I've got you. Christian, let go. I've got you. People, let go. I've got you."

CUSTODIAN, NOT JANITOR

A janitor is "one who keeps the premises clean, tends the

heating system, and makes minor repairs." The Holy Spirit has sometimes been regarded as a holy janitor. He is named as part of the Trinity, but given a minor role. If "janitor" sounds discourteous, he could be named a "sacristan," one who is in charge of the sacristy and ceremonial equipment. This would come close to the idea of relegating him to what we called a "gilded cage." But he is not satisfied with keeping the church tidy or at a comfortable temperature (remember Jesus prefers his church to be hot or cold, not lukewarm). He excels in major overhauls, not just minor repairs.

"Custodian" is a better word for the Holy Spirit. A custodian is "one who is charged with guarding and keeping." That's a more proper job description for the Spirit. That's what Jesus had in mind when his earthly presence was exchanged for the omnipresence of his Spirit. Protection and maintenance continue to be his chief tasks in the church.

Chapters 14-16 of John's Gospel were our basis for "The Holy Spirit calls." The book of Acts, especially chapters 2 and 4, emphasized the Spirit's work of gathering. We focused upon 1st Corinthians, chapter 12, to see how he enlightens us with his gifts. His sanctifying work was highlighted by the list of spiritual fruits of the Spirit found in Galatians 5:22-23. For our present purpose, we turn to Romans, chapter 8. It is the most concentrated portion of scripture dealing with the keeping activity of the Holy Spirit.

THE HOLY SPIRIT KEEPS US FORGIVEN AND FORGIVING

Guilt condemns. Forgiveness frees. Sinful condition and choices led to death as consequence - that was the "law of sin and death." But a new law became an option. Paul calls this the "law of the Spirit of life in Christ Jesus" (Romans 8:2). Sin and death were marked by an independence from God, or, more really, a rebellion against him. The Spirit-led life is one of dependence, that is, dependence upon what God accomplished in Jesus. It was the original "Master Charge." God agreed to credit his Son's life and death to the debit account of anyone who accepted this gracious offer. God then marked that account "Paid in Full." The consequence of this new arrangement was good news: "There is therefore now no condemnation for those who are in Christ Jesus" (Romans 8:1). Setting the mind on the Spirit is life and peace (Romans 8:6) because it includes the assuring recollection of Jesus' completed sacrifice for all our sins.

The Spirit keeps us forgiving, as well as forgiven. Life right now has the aroma of resurrection about it (Romans 8:11) because newness reigns. This includes new attitudes and inclinations. It includes a whole new wardrobe, in fact, as Paul describes it in Colossians 3:12. "Put on, then, as God's chosen ones, holy and beloved, compassion, kindness, lowliness, meekness, and patience, forbearing one another and, if one has a complaint against another, forgiving each other; as the Lord has forgiven you, so you also must forgive." It is the Spirit who empowers the chain reaction of forgiven/forgiving.

THE HOLY SPIRIT KEEPS US IN GOD'S FAMILY

"For all who are led by the Spirit of God are sons of God. For you did not receive the spirit of slavery to fall back into fear, but you have received the spirit of sonship. When we cry, 'Abba! Father!' it is the Spirit himself bearing witness with our spirit that we are children of God" (Romans 8:14-16).

Relationship is stronger stuff than fellowship. Pauline and I have three boys who are our sons. There is nothing that will change that. The relationship is secure. We are stuck with each other! The relationship is not on-again, off-again. It is and always shall be on.

Daily fellowship, however, develops wrinkles. There may be spats, misunderstandings, outright obstinacy. These interruptions in fellowship are not unimportant. They need to be dealt with. Communion has to be restored. Feelings require first aid. Trust levels may need to be recovered. But none of these problems have disenfranchised our sons. The relationship remains unchanged during the breaks in fellowship.

The Holy Spirit maintains the relationship between God

and his children. Part of his keeping power is to sustain within us a grateful confidence in a loving heavenly Father who has made us part of his family. It is an evil spirit that tempts us into thinking that God is capricious, and that we can never be sure just where we stand with him. No earthly parents would want their children to live in such insecurity; neither does our heavenly Father.

At the same time that he maintains the relationship, the Holy Spirit services the fellowship between God and his children. To be prompted toward repentance when we have sinned is a merciful act of the Spirit. To call us back from straying is his loving duty. To know a reassuring touch from the Father of us all is a refreshing experience. To go to sleep at night with the peace and assurance of the Lord's forgiveness, loving concern and watchful care is the best medicine for a good rest.

The Spirit is no grumpy nanny who keeps us in line as God's harshly disciplined children. Rather, he rejoices to keep us in line in another way, that is, to keep us in line for an ever greater future as children in God's family. "If children, then heirs, heirs of God and fellow heirs with Christ, provided we suffer with him in order that we may also be glorified with him" (Romans 8:17).

THE HOLY SPIRIT KEEPS US CONTENT

Suffering as God's children is not an option. It is a guarantee. No family is without times of trial and tears. But the Holy Spirit is active to sustain us through the bad times as well as to give us rejoicing spirits when good occurs. The endurance of suffering begins with a right mind-set. Paul exhibited such a conviction when he wrote: "I consider that our present sufferings are not worth comparing with the glory that will be revealed in us" (Romans 8:18, NIV).

When I see this conviction currently operating in the lives of sufferers, I feel as though I should stand and salute them. They are today's heroes of the faith. I will let the mention of one couple represent a host of such heroes. Twenty years ago, the husband suffered a hard stroke that at first was deemed terminal. Recovery has been far from miraculous. Speech is unintelligible to most. Movement is severely limited. Each day brings a repeat of difficult routines for the wife to perform and the husband to endure. They don't make a pretense about their situation. It is grueling business. But they have not lost an authentic gratitude for life, a joy in togetherness, and a contagious sense of humor. What most basically sustains them is a continuing conviction that God cares, and that their future is exciting because of the Lord's sure promises. Only the Spirit's daily ministration keeps them strangely content amidst suffering. They join the creation standing on tiptoes as they await the time they will "be set free from its bondage to decay and obtain the glorious liberty of the children of God" (Romans 8:21).

Keep this couple in mind as Paul continues: "We know that the whole creation has been groaning in travail together until now; and not only the creation, but we ourselves, who have the first fruits of the Spirit, groan inwardly as we wait for adoption as sons, the redemption of our bodies. For in this hope we were saved" (Romans 8:22-24a).

THE HOLY SPIRIT KEEPS US LEANING

The church is one great leaning society. When I am up and things are going well, other brothers and sisters in difficult situations can lean upon me. My faith can be more optimistic on their behalf. My prayers can be more positive. But the time will come when I am down and they are up. It is now my turn to lean on them. Just when I need to pray the most, I often feel least like praying. How good it is to relax in those moments, not give in to attacks of guilt, and be buoyed up by the concern and support of other believers who are representing me and my needs before the Father.

There is also someone else who invites me to be a leaner. "Likewise the Spirit helps us in our weakness; for we do not know how to pray as we ought, but the Spirit himself intercedes for us with sighs too deep for words. And he who searches the hearts of men knows what is the mind of the Spirit, because the Spirit intercedes for the saints according to the will of God" (Romans 8:26-27). We pray the best when we pray the worst. When we are at a loss for words and the only expression of need is our heartache, the Spirit goes to bat for us. Spiritual gifts of discernment and interpretation take place at top level, in the very Godhead. The result is a perfect request to the Father on our behalf, a prayer for us that is absolutely in line with God's will. God is so merciful that he turns our worst prayers into the best prayers! There is surprising strength that comes from being a leaner, and the Holy Spirit keeps us leaning upon him, and upon one another.

THE HOLY SPIRIT KEEPS US SECURE

No theological squabbling should rob a Christian of his sense of security, especially his eternal security. There is, to be sure, a mental wrestling match in store for those who grapple with the idea of double predestination, that is, whether God destines some to salvation and others to condemnation. There is also the chance that people will give the matter of "once saved/always saved" a quarter turn and make of it a reason to presume God's love in spite of their personal desires to wander and squander their lives.

There are plenty temptations to do mental meanderings, but their outcome is never as helpful as what results when concentration is given to the sure promises of God in his word. No surer promises are given than the words of Romans 8:28-30. There is security in knowing that "in everything God works for good with those who love him." There is security in the uninterrupted progression of "predestined-called-justi-fied- glorified" in verse 30. A sense of security always has to reside in what God is like. We know ourselves too well to root such security in what we are or do. The sheep are never the source of security that the Shepherd is. Jesus repeated himself for our benefit when he said "..and I give them (my sheep) eternal life, and they shall never perish, and no one shall snatch them out of my hand. My Father, who has given them to me, is greater than all, and no one is able to snatch them out of the Father's hand" (John 10:28-29). While the future of Social Security is questionable and the issue of national security is both debatable and risky, God offers an unmatched eternal security that is too often neglected in the general pursuit of lesser concerns.

I once cut out an ad that promised one year of Eternity for a very low price! It was, of course, a commercial for a magazine. Yet without the Holy Spirit applying God's truth in our hearts, we would live under the illusion that we have to pay for some kind of subscription to eternity. It is the Holy Spirit who keeps us trusting; not in ourselves, but in what the Lord has done for us so we can be assured of an eternity with him. "On the last day He will raise me and all the dead and give me and all believers in Christ eternal life. This is most certainly true." (Luther's Small Catechism)

THE HOLY SPIRIT KEEPS US "VICTORS PLUS"

How can we be "more than conquerors" (Romans 8:37)? Conquerors would seem to be at the top of the pile. But conquerors have had to fight their own battles. To have the benefit of victory without paying the price of waging the war is to be more than conquerors. The enemies are big-timers and the list is long: tribulation, distress, persecution, famine, nakedness, peril, sword, death, life, angels, principalities, things present or future, powers, height, depth, anything in creation. There will be scars from the battle. We may be knocked down, but not out. The prize would be whisked out of our grip if we alone held it. But when the tag team of sin, death and the devil was about to be declared winner, another entered the ring. God did not spare his own Son, but enlisted him in the contest. The tide was turned. Sin lost its power, death its stranglehold, and the devil his territorial reign. The life, death, and resurrection of Jesus entitled him to wear the crown of victory, but he has chosen to share it instead of wear it. A strange coronation takes place. When the Spirit brings us to confess "Jesus is Lord," a crown is placed on *our heads*! By sustaining us in that confession, the Holy Spirit keeps us in the status of "victors plus."

FINDER/KEEPER

On my desk are several bowls of variously shaped and colored stones. They seem without value and appear to just add to the clutter. But I found those stones. There was a moment of joy in each separate discovery. I would have difficulty taking them out on the deck and throwing them into the forest. I am their keeper as well as their finder. No one else has that unique stance toward them.

The Holy Spirit is our finder and keeper. His task did not end with calling us, but led to the further involvements of gathering, enlightening and sanctifying. His job of keeping us will end only as he ushers each of us safely into the unending presence of the Father in heaven.

My mother had a broach with many little stones in it. Once when I was looking through her jewelry box, I asked her why she never wore that broach. She said that a stone was missing. Upon closer examination, I discovered one empty setting. There were many remaining, but the one missing stone took the joy out of wearing the broach.

I like to think that God has a majestic crown with a unique stone for every person he has created and included in his plan of salvation. If that plan is frustrated, a stone is missing for each person who does not experience a God-intended eternity. God the Father sees the missing stones, and his heart is made sad. The Holy Spirit knows this and is thus impelled on his errand of finding and keeping each precious jewel.

> "Little children, little children
> Who love their Redeemer
> Are the jewels, precious jewels,
> His loved, and his own.
> Like the stars of the morning
> His bright crown adorning,
> They shall shine in their beauty,
> Bright gems for his crown."
> (Swedish children's hymn)

* * *

Note the "Think/Talk/Pray about" section relating to Chapter 8.

CHAPTER NINE

The Holy Spirit in the Life of the Believer

THE FLUENCY OF THE HOLY SPIRIT

The dictionary definition of "fluency" is "the quality of moving freely." It is therefore a good word to use in describing the action of the Holy Spirit.

The wind has this quality of moving freely. Jesus said, "The wind blows where it wills, and you hear the sound of it, but you do not know whence it comes or whither it goes; so it is with every one who is born of the Spirit" (John 3:8).

I suppose there were times when people had no concept of this force that could stir up and even destroy things. They would only take cover and be fearful until the wind died down. There are people who are also apprehensive about the movement of the Holy Spirit. They would like to cage or control him. Being unable to do this, they would relax more if this spiritual wind died down and allowed the return of a quiet, even deadly, calm.

Still others are presumptuous enough to act like a person standing out in a strong wind, waving arms and giving signals, as though able to direct the course of the wind and coerce it to accomplish preset tasks.

Both the person who is apprehensive about the action of the Holy Spirit and the person who enthusiastically insists that the Spirit act in prescribed ways upon others make the same mistake. They overlook the fluency of the Spirit, his

81

quality of moving freely. They forget that the wind blows where it wills and that the Spirit acts "as he wills" (1st Cor. 12:11).

INFLUENCED BY THE HOLY SPIRIT

Originally, the word "influence" meant "a flow of ethereal fluid believed to emanate from the stars and to affect human actions." Since such ethereal fluid is rather hard to come by, there have been plenty substitutes made available. If you see anyone who is "under the influence" nowadays, it is traceable to man-made spirits rather than some kind of heavenly fluid!

Paul knew that the people in Ephesus would get his message when he used the contrast recorded in the fifth chapter. "Do not get drunk with wine, for that is debauchery; but be filled with the Spirit" (Ephesians 5:18). It was not the first time that this connection had been made. When the Holy Spirit first came upon the disciples at Pentecost, the world's diagnosis was that they were "under the influence." Peter had to explain, "These men are not drunk, as you suppose, since it is only the third hour of the day" (Acts 2:15). Then he went on to point out the promise by the prophet Joel that God would pour out his Spirit and people would come under his influence. "And it shall come to pass afterward, that I will pour out my spirit on all flesh; your sons and your daughters shall prophesy, your old men shall dream dreams, and your young men shall see visions. Even upon the menservants and maidservants in those days, I will pour out my spirit" (Joel 2:28-29).

While the world wondered what had come over the believers at Pentecost, the disciples themselves realized that it was their Lord keeping a promise he had made to them. "You shall receive power when the Holy Spirit has come upon you; and you shall be my witnesses" (Acts 1:8).

Wine does have its own way of lowering inhibitions and making a person bolder and louder than usual. But God has a better idea. Drunkenness and lies go together; the Spirit is the Spirit of Truth. Strong drink curses; the Spirit brings blessing. It would be interesting to get a recovered alcoholic and a Spirit-excited Christian together to teach a lesson on Ephesians 5:18!

INFLUENZA AND THE SPIRIT

A dictionary defines "influenza" as "an acute, infectious disease, probably caused by a specific bacterium and frequently occurring in epidemic form, characterized by inflammation of the air passages, severe muscular pains and headache, digestive and nervous disturbances, and prostration: often followed by serious after effects: popularly called flu." (Winston University Dictionary)

The Holy Spirit has not only been mistakenly labeled as drunkenness. He has also been diagnosed as a type of influenza - Holy Spirit Flu! It appears infectious; it presents the danger of epidemic; it causes pain and upset. There is often evidence of nervous disturbance, and there are sometimes serious aftereffects.

Though the Holy Spirit has been blamed or credited for a variety of ailments not of his doing, St. Paul says that even the authentic activity of the Spirit is misinterpreted. "The man without the Spirit does not accept the things that come from the Spirit of God, for they are foolishness to him, and he cannot understand them, because they are spiritually discerned" (1st Cor.2:14, NIV). A lady told me about a letter she received in which the writer said, "The kind of Christianity practiced by many is so cold that when someone becomes normal, they think he has a fever!"

I must admit that I have at times felt threatened and uneasy about signs of renewal and revival around me. What is alarming is that I must ask myself whether my point of reference is a sick church or a well one. Read the whole of Romans 12. If it describes a healthy church, then much of the church today is sick. The sickness is not caused by the Holy Spirit; but the Holy Spirit can cure it!

HOLY SPIRIT AFFLUENCE

Affluence is no stranger to us. If we get hungry, it is

because we are too busy to eat, not because the cupboard is bare. If we are cold, we likely have forgotten any of four or five coats or sweaters in the closet. We know physical affluence, that is, abundance of material things.

Paul writes in Romans 14:17, "The kingdom of God does not mean food and drink but righteousness and peace and joy in the Holy Spirit." Here is the affluent God piling the spiritual tables full of good things.

Paul didn't pray for a stuffy church, but he did pray for a stuffed one. Note his words: "May the God of hope *fill* you with *all* joy and peace in believing, so that by the power of the Holy Spirit you may *abound* in hope. I myself am satisfied about you, my brethren, that you yourselves are *full* of goodness, *filled* with *all* knowledge, and able to instruct one another" (Romans 15:13-14).

The Holy Spirit is the supply agent for the church. He gives the power tools or gifts meant to build up the church (1st Cor. 12:1-6). He is the power source (Acts 1:8) adequate for the task of carving the kingdom of God out of rough stones found in the world. The resulting living temple shows what Holy Spirit skill can do under a handicap! Then he landscapes in a lavish display of fruit (Gal. 5:22-23). If we are not experiencing the affluence of the Holy Spirit, it is because we are neglecting the tools, not appropriating the power, and not trusting for the results.

The affluence of the Holy Spirit is in keeping with the Father's affluence in creating and sustaining the world and the Son's affluence in redeeming it.

INFLUENCE— THE INWARD FLOW OF THE SPIRIT

"Fluency," and other words related to it, appeals to me as a helpful term to use in connection with the Holy Spirit because it allows for looking at his ministry from a directional point of view.

"Affluence" really means to "flow toward." We have already mentioned the Spirit's initiating movement toward believers. "Influence" offers another directional insight. It suggests the "inflow" of the Holy Spirit. A related definition of influence is also easily connected to the Holy Spirit's activity, namely, "power tending to produce effects by indirect or invisible means."

Think of how the Samaritan woman at the well was influenced during her encounter with Jesus. She knew only one kind of water, the kind you could see and feel and swallow. She had yet to learn about a water that quenched a soul thirst. A drink of this strange water promised the start of an inner flowing well that would assure a constant supply (John 4:13-14).

Farmers and ranchers are utterly dependent upon snowfall and rainfall for prosperity, if not survival. They cannot dig their own wells sufficient for their needs. Some have learned a trust that keeps them content and secure. Others remain worried and anxious until the grain is in the bin; then it's time to begin worrying about the next crop.

Christians, especially church leaders, can identify with farmers at this point. They may experience a gnawing anxiety about spiritually running dry. They may become frustrated with the responsibility of always having to produce. But they may also learn a relaxed trust in one who has promised and provided a drink that both quenches personal soul thirst and becomes a source of living water adequate for any ministry to others. The Holy Spirit supervises this vital inflow.

EFFLUENCE - THE OUTWARD FLOW OF THE SPIRIT.

Affluence - to flow toward in abundance.

Influence - To flow in with effective power.

Effluence - to flow out like a stream from a lake.

In John's Gospel, Jesus gives this promise to any believer: "Out of his heart shall flow rivers of living water." Then the gospel writer explains, "Now this he said about the Spirit" (John 7:38-39). This flow is not meant to be only into a private watering hole. The living water is not meant to be capped, or stored up in some reservoir where it will become stagnant. If the flow of the gospel is just into the believer, the Spirit's work is only half done. Disciples were never meant to get so full of the good news that they begin to choke on it. They are meant to overflow. It is this effluent aspect of the Holy Spirit's ministry that must become more and more evident throughout the church.

I once found a pastor practicing an illustration for his next sermon. He asked me to watch the demonstration and critique it. He had a card table on which he had placed a variety of empty water glasses. He also had a large bag full of marbles. To show how love was to overflow from the life of every Christian, he planned to fill the glasses with marbles until they began to spill out. However, as he began the practice demonstration, the bag broke. Marbles rolled all over the chancel, down the aisles, and under the pews. As we were picking them up, I assured him that it was a good illustration for Sunday.. as long as he didn't lose all his marbles!

Effluence, outflow, is an exciting aspect of the Holy Spirit's ministry. The hearer of the gospel becomes a bearer of the gospel. The person who comes to know the peace of God in Christ becomes an instrument of that peace. Those who have had Christian love shown to them begin to exercise it with lips and life toward others. People who have tended to stop with trusting Jesus for salvation go on to trust the Holy Spirit for sanctification. The branch no longer simply takes its life from the vine; it starts to bear the fruits of the Spirit.

We live on the fulfillment side of John 7:39. "Now this he (Jesus) said about the Spirit, which those who believed in him were to receive; for as yet the Spirit had not been given, because Jesus was not yet glorified." The Spirit has now been given. Though the rainbow is God's promise that ordinary water will never again be unleashed to destroy the earth, God's Spirit is his promise to bring a deluge of living water flowing in and through disciples as a way of blessing and refreshing the world.

AVOIDING THE EFFLUVIAL

It happened in Cairo, Egypt. We went into a perfume

shop. The proprietor asked us to be seated in a circle. Persian carpets were on the floor and draped over the couches. When the owner gave the signal, many helpers came carrying bottles of very special perfumes. As the fragrances were described to us, the helpers came around and rubbed samples on our arms. We soon had so many samples that we couldn't tell or smell one from the other. We had to admit, however, that there was not a bad fragrance among them.

What does this have to do with the fluency of the Holy Spirit? One related word is the adjective "effluvial." It means "pertaining to an especially disagreeable odor, as one coming from decaying matter." We take from it a word of caution. The witness produced by the Holy Spirit is not an effluvial one. If a person witnesses only about how he was saved thirty years ago, there may be a stale, musty smell to it. If one just tells and retells a past experience of being filled with the Holy Spirit, the living water will seem more like a stagnant pool.

What people in and out of the church need is the aroma of our witness to the "now" meaning of Christ in our lives. What the world needs is the fragrance of our present and daily dependence upon and experience of the Holy Spirit of God.

The church is meant to be like that perfume shop. The action of Father, Son, and Spirit upon each individual is so unique that every person contributes to the fragrance spread by the church (2nd Cor 2:14). Such variety of fragrance need not invite competition or condemnation, and any comparisons may be made with kindness. Together, "we are the aroma of Christ" (2 Cor. 2:15).

*   *   *

Note the "Think/Talk/Pray about" section relating to
Chapter 9.

*T*hink...Talk...
Pray About

CHAPTER 1 ......IT'S A BIRD!

1. Which of the following describe your familiarity, or unfamiliarity, with the Holy Spirit? Explain your answer.
   a. "the least understood member of the Trinity"
   b. "more like an 'it' than a 'He'"
   c. "spotlights the Father and the Son, so the Holy Spirit is appropriately more obscure"
   d. "a daily presence and power in my life"
2. Check the liturgy of Confirmation (for Lutherans, Lutheran Book of Worship pp. 200-201). Note its Spirit-centeredness. If you have been confirmed, do you remember it as a Spirit-centered experience? Discuss what seemed most prominent about your confirmation.
3. Do "gilded" and "gifted" cages represent a fair general appraisal of the treatment of the Holy Spirit in sacramental and pentecostal traditions? What seems right or wrong about such cages?
4. What has been your reaction, or the reaction of others, toward more recent increased interest in the ministry of the Holy Spirit (give examples):
   - Apprehension?
   - Titillation?
   - Calm assessment?
5. Talk about how attitudes toward God the Father and God

the Son can be clues regarding proper or improper attitudes toward God the Holy Spirit. For example, acceptance... availability... pursuit...coercion... control... gratitude... personal closeness.

6. Share new insights/understanding gained from this chapter.

CHAPTER 2 ......IT'S A PAIN!

1. New spiritual insights or experiences may be called "moments of meaning." Have you had any that brought both blessing and bewilderment? Share examples.

2. "Competition" means "a contest between rivals." "Complementary" means "mutually supplying each other's needs." A congregation or fellowship group is composed of individuals with a variety of background, preference, and spiritual experience. Should such variety be viewed as "competition" or as "complementary"? Why?

3. Diagnose some pains using the following outline:

Congregational Pastoral Individual

Example of pain:
Negative aspects:
Positive potential:

4."The ultimate target of our impatience is God himself." What is your reaction to this statement? Share any instances where you have had to choose between being restless about a matter (impatience) and resting in the Lord (trust).

5. Share new insights/understanding gained from this chapter.

CHAPTER 3 ......THE HOLY SPIRIT IN THE LIFE OF JESUS

1."The Father and the Son are the friends; the Holy Spirit is the stranger." Is this observation a fair statement about the level of familiarity with the members of the Trinity in the church today? What are some reasons for your answer?

2. Jesus did not say or do things on his own but as empow-

ered by the Spirit. How does this make his incarnation and humanity more real?

3. "Event alone becomes history; relationship is current event." How does this apply to the daily meaning of baptism?

4. The divinity of Jesus can be emphasized in a way that detracts from the reality of his humanity. Cite some biblical studies or personal experiences in which Jesus' humanity may have been written off or taken less seriously because of his divine nature.

5. How do you react to the thought that the Holy Spirit is as available to empower you to do God's will as he was to Jesus? Does that thought create excitement? Apprehension? Doubt? Awe?

6. Share new insights/understanding gained from this chapter.

CHAPTER 4 ......THE HOLY SPIRIT CALLS

1. Who, or what, has been a channel by which you have heard the good news of Jesus and his love? Tell about it. Have you ever thanked someone for being such a channel? Would such attention be an embarrassment or an encouragement?

2. List some ways that the three persons of the Trinity offer the church examples of cooperation instead of competition, commendation rather than criticism, unity without uniformity.

3. A Russian proverb says "Accept our hospitality, but tell the truth." How might this be applied to congregational fellowship? Have you practiced or observed casual delusion within the church? How has it made the church less effective and less helpful?

4. "The Spirit recognizes himself not only within a believer, but between believers." How have you experienced the truth of this statement?

5. Reflect upon some coincidence in your life and see how it may have been better described as a "God-incident."

6. How does being a witness sound less threatening than being a salesperson?

7. Share new insights/understanding gained from this chapter.

CHAPTER 5 ......THE HOLY SPIRIT GATHERS

1. Imagine that every member of every Christian congregation had "an infectious desire to be together with others who reverenced Jesus as Lord." What would be some of the results?
2. There is so much pressure to succeed, excel and be "Number One." Can you think of instances where failure or disappointment has bound people closer together than success has been able to do? Share examples.
3. Consider "intentional gathering." Who are some people you know who have this motivation? Think of a meeting or event that exemplifies intentional gathering. Can you detect anything unique about such a meeting? About those who attend?
4. Under the following headings, list examples of the various kinds of happenings:
   Fellowship (Koinonia)
   Service (Diakonia)
   Proclamation (Kerygma)
5. Share new insights/understanding gained from this chapter.

CHAPTER 6 ......THE HOLY SPIRIT
ENLIGHTENS

1. Take some time to honestly assess gifts evident in your life and in others around you. Most people need the help and encouragement of others in order to become sensitive to their own strengths and talents.
2. Review the biblical references to spiritual gifts in Jesus' life. Discuss whether they make proper and accurate connections to the gifts listed in 1st Corinthians 12. Do they validate the place of spiritual gifts in the experience of Christians today? Explain your reaction.
3. "The gifts are for service, not for status." Does this statement place the gifts in proper perspective? Why or why not? Share some examples of service use or status use of spiritual gifts.
4. An old hymn says "Tis a gift to be simple." How might simple appreciation be better than complicated reasoning when considering the gifts of the Spirit?

5.   Share new insights/understanding gained from this chapter.

CHAPTER 7 ......THE HOLY SPIRIT SANCTIFIES

1. Share new insights/understanding gained from this chapter.

2. Instead of having many questions to discuss, use your time to give attention to the matter of "Trusting versus Trying."

One woman's story: "For 16 years I harped at my daughter about keeping her room clean. Finally I told the Lord 'I am releasing this whole situation to you. It is beyond me.' And for the first time in her life, my daughter began keeping her room clean without my nagging at her."

Another woman's story: "During the first 25 years of our marriage, my husband never closed a drawer that he pulled open. I always had bruises from bumping into open drawers. Then I got to the point where I said 'Lord, I give up. You'll have to take over, because I have gotten nowhere trying to change this habit of his.' Five years have gone by since I prayed that prayer — and my husband has never stopped leaving drawers open!"

Do we have only one success story here, or two? Results cannot be guaranteed when attitudes and actions of other people are involved. We cannot reach into their lives and press buttons that insure immediate and exact results to our liking. Actually, both women were successful in that they both quit trying and started trusting. Even without similar happy endings, they both found freedom from the pressure of being another person's life changer. Only God is equipped for such a task.

Think of a situation you have been trying to control. In your mind, back off and observe that situation. Realize your attempts to manage and orchestrate people and events. Repent for having been too presumptuous about your own power to alter and direct them. Confess that you are powerless, helpless, ineffective. In that confession, let there be a knowing that a power transfer has taken place. God has not been unconcerned, but he can now be even more involved. He has been hampered, not helped, by your past determination to be adequate in this case.

Know a peace about the future. Be willing to only wait. Trusting is neither fruitless nor a waste of time. What you need most has already come to you; that is, a new sense of relief since you no longer are under the pressure of producing what you cannot supply, and a new confidence that the matter will resolve best in God's hands.

There may be more than one area in your life where you need to let trusting replace trying. Christian sharing can be a help and encouragement in this adventure.

CHAPTER 8 ......THE HOLY SPIRIT KEEPS

1. As a way of updating your confirmation or renewing a "letting go" openness to the Holy Spirit, pray this personalized form of some parts of the Confirmation liturgy:

"Gracious Lord, through water and the Spirit you have made me your own. You forgave me all my sins and brought me to newness of life. Continue to strengthen me with the Holy Spirit, and daily increase in me your gifts of grace: the spirit of wisdom and understanding, the spirit of counsel and might, the spirit of knowledge and the fear of the Lord, the spirit of joy in your presence; through Jesus Christ, your Son, my Lord.

"Father in heaven, for Jesus' sake, stir up in me the gift of your Holy Spirit; confirm my faith, guide my life, empower me in my serving, give me patience in suffering, and bring me to everlasting life. Amen."

God takes this prayer seriously and is eager to answer it (See Luke 11:11-13). Do not be surprised at new awareness and evidence of the Holy Spirit's presence and power in your life after such a prayer.

2. "The Spirit keeps me forgiving, as well as forgiven." Which is most difficult for you: to forgive, or to accept forgiveness? Why? Think of some person toward whom you will right this moment, in your mind and heart, consciously exercise a willingness to forgive. Be aware of a freedom from resentment in the matter. Resentment flees when forgiveness frees.

3. How does it help to think of your life with God in terms of a relationship that endures, along with a fellowship that needs repeated mending?

4. Share how you have experienced the church as being a "mutual leaning society."

5. Share new insights/understanding gained from this chapter.

CHAPTER 9 ......THE HOLY SPIRIT IN
THE LIFE OF THE BELIEVER

1. How might the phrase "free as the wind" contribute to understanding the action of the Holy Spirit
- in the life of an individual believer?
- in the fellowship of a Christian congregation?
- in our attitude toward other denominations?

2. Do the suggested exercise. "Read the whole of Romans 12. If it describes a healthy church, then much of the church today is sick. The sickness is not caused by the Holy Spirit; but the Holy Spirit can cure it!" Discuss the conclusions in these last two sentences. Which of the many admonitions of St. Paul do you think are most important to heed today.

3. "Inflow" and "outflow" are used to picture the ministry of the Holy Spirit in the life of the believer. Do you perceive a greater need for one or the other in your life? In your church? Explain.

4. Share new insights/understanding gained from this chapter.

5. Has the Holy Spirit become a friendlier, more personal reality to you through these chapters? If so, tell him that in your own words. He will be heartened, and the Father and Son will share his joy.